LIGHT JOURNEY

Encountering Saints, Miracles, and Sacred Places

ROBERT JOHN HAMMOND

Light Journey: Encountering Saints, Miracles, and Sacred Places
Copyright © 2025 Robert Hammond

All rights reserved. This book may not be reproduced, in whole or in part, in any form or by any means electronic or mechanical, including photocopying, recording, or by any information storage and retrieval system now or hereafter invented, without written permission of the publisher, New Way Press. For reproduction rights or questions email info@newwaypress.com.

ISBN: 979-8-9919293-0-1

Published by:
  New Way Press
  http://www.NewWayPress.com
  Sacramento, CA 95835

Cover photo by Gillfoto, CC BY-SA 3.0 <https://creativecommons.org/licenses/by-sa/3.0>, via Wikimedia Commons

Printed in the United States of America

Acknowledgments

Special thanks to my wife, Lesa, who read and reread all the drafts of this book and provided valuable suggestions, clarification, and feedback.

Many thanks to Archbishop Benjamin, Fr. Timothy Winegar, and Fr. Ian MacKinnon for their blessing, encouragement and prayers. Thank you to Christine Gindi for her relentless support, encouragement, and assistance. Thanks also to Katherine Hyde for her professional editorial comments and assistance. Thank you to Father Marko Bojovic of Saint Sava Serbian Orthodox Church for your insights on interviews about Saint Sebastian of Jackson. Thank you to Silas Karbo, Theodosius Santalov, and Robin Innokentia Wellman for helping to make the *American Orthodox* film a reality.

Above all, thanks to God and All Saints of North America for shining the Light and guiding the Way.

Contents

Acknowledgments	3
Preface	7
Introduction: A Modern Pilgrimage	13
The Iveron Icon of the Mother of God	17
The Night of Souls	23
Fort Ross and the Seeds of Orthodoxy	31
St. John the Wonderworker of San Francisco	41
St. Sebastian of Jackson: The American Missionary	51
The Spiritual Fathers and Mothers of America: Saints Raphael, Alexis Toth, John Kochurov of Chicago, and Olga Michael of Alaska	59
Father Seraphim Rose: The Quiet Fire	67
Brother Jose Muñoz: Guardian of the Myrrh-Streaming Icon	75
Elder Ephraim of Arizona : The Spiritual Builder	87
The Native American Journey to Orthodoxy: Finding Faith in the Ancient Church	97
The African American Experience: A Path to Orthodoxy	111

The Art and Architecture of Orthodox America	131
Holy Places and Pilgrimage in America	139
The Future of Orthodoxy in America	151
Epilogue: Continuing the Pilgrimage	155
Appendix: A Guide to Pilgrimage Sites and Holy Places in America	159
About the Author	165

Preface

The road winds northward along the California Coast Highway, curling its way along the edge of the Pacific. To my left, the ocean stretches endlessly, its restless waves crashing against the weathered cliffs below. The salty breeze seeps through the cracks around the car window, mingling with the faint scent of pine from the thick forest on the right. As the sun begins to set, casting a golden hue over the horizon, the highway twists and turns, each bend revealing a new vista more breathtaking than the last. My hands grip the steering wheel, steady and sure, but my heart races with the anticipation of the journey ahead.

I am on my way to Fort Ross, a place of history and holiness, a place where the stories of the saints and martyrs of Orthodoxy in America first began to unfold. The road seems to pull me forward, as if the land itself is drawing me to this sacred ground. I pass by ancient redwoods, their trunks towering like silent sentinels, and I am reminded that I am one of many travelers who have come this way before, searching for something beyond the ordinary, something that speaks to the soul.

As the ancient wooden fort comes into view, its weathered walls standing defiantly against the encroaching wilderness, I see familiar faces—friends, fellow Orthodox parishioners, clergy, pilgrims, and a documentary film crew—all gathered here, united by a common purpose. We have come to tell the story of the saints who transformed America, to bear witness to the miracles and the living faith that continue to shape our lives. I park the car and step out, feeling the crunch of gravel underfoot and the cool breeze on my face. I am filled with a sense of gratitude for this moment, this gathering, this journey.

I'm not young enough to know everything. There was a time when I thought I did—when I was convinced that I had all the answers, that my youthful passion and zeal could change the world. Growing up in the late sixties, amid social upheaval and revolution, I embraced the rebellious spirit of the age. "Never trust anybody over thirty" was the slogan of my generation, a rallying cry that seemed to capture all the fervor and idealism of our youth. We were convinced that we were the ones who would remake the world, that we had no need for the wisdom of our elders or the traditions of the past.

But as I have grown older, I have come to see the folly of that arrogance, that divide-and-conquer attitude that only served to inflame our pride, vanity, jealousy, anger, and every other passion that clouded our minds and hearts. I realize now how much I was shaped by the very forces I thought I was resisting. The slogans and mantras of my youth, which once seemed so liberating, now appear as chains that bound me in ignorance and self-deception.

Preface

"Honor thy father and mother" is a phrase that has come to mean something very different to me now. I no longer see it as a commandment or a rebuke but as a reminder of the importance of humility, of recognizing that I am just one link in a long chain of believers who have come before me. It is a call to respect my elders, to listen to the wisdom of the Church Fathers, hierarchs, parents, godparents, and the older men and women who walked this path of faith long before I set foot on it.

In seeking to develop an Orthodox way of thinking—what the Church Fathers call *phronema*—I am still learning to see the world not through the lens of my own desires and ambitions, but through the eyes of those who have gone before me. I am learning to approach the mysteries of the faith with a sense of awe and reverence, to seek guidance not in my own limited understanding but in the teachings and traditions of the Church, passed down through the centuries.

This book comes out of my desire to honor those who have come before me, those who know much more than I will ever know. I am grateful to the historians, the scholars, the saints, and the Fathers of the Church who, despite my small comprehension, continue to shine the light of wisdom for the modern world and offer guidance to the world to come.

I wrote this book to leave behind a glimpse of the things that I have seen and come to know, even though, as St. Paul says, "through a glass, darkly." I do not pretend to have all the answers, nor do I claim to have fully grasped the depth and breadth of the Orthodox faith. I am but a humble pilgrim, trying to capture the beauty of the journey, the wonder of the saints, the miracles, and the living faith that continue to shape and sustain us.

As we gather here at Fort Ross, I am struck by the sense of continuity, the unbroken line that connects us to those early missionaries who brought the Orthodox faith to this land. I think of St. Herman of Alaska, St. Peter the Aleut, and St. John the Wonderworker of San Francisco—saints who lived and died on this soil, whose lives were marked by humility, sacrifice, and unwavering faith. Their stories, their examples, are the foundation on which we continue to build. Their lives remind us that Orthodoxy is not just a faith of the past but a living, breathing reality that continues to transform hearts and minds.

This book is a small attempt to tell those stories, to shine a light on the saints and miracles that have shaped the Orthodox Church in America. It is an invitation to join me on this journey, to explore the rich tapestry of faith, culture, and history that makes Orthodoxy in America such a unique and vibrant expression of the Christian faith.

Please forgive me in advance for all that I have not properly communicated or comprehended. I am aware of my limitations, aware that I can only scratch the surface of these wonderful and amazing stories. But I hope that in these pages, you will find something that speaks to your own heart, something that draws you closer to the saints, to the Church, and ultimately, to Christ Himself.

The evening sun dips low, its golden rays slipping over the walls of the fort, and a calm settles within me, like the quieting of a distant sea. I look around at the faces of my fellow pilgrims and feel a connection that goes beyond words, beyond time and space. We are here, in this moment, because we are part of a story that is much larger than ourselves—a story that began long before we were born and will continue long after we are gone. It is a story of faith, of miracles, of a living God who is still at work in the world today.

May this book be a small offering in that great story, a humble contribution to the ongoing narrative of Orthodoxy in America. May it inspire you to seek the good, the true, and the beautiful, to honor those who have come before us, and to continue the journey of faith with humility, courage, and love.

Introduction

A MODERN PILGRIMAGE

The wind rushes through the pines, a low, mournful whisper that sways the tall trees standing like sentinels along the mountain ridge. A lone figure moves along the narrow path, careful not to trip on the roots that twist out of the earth like gnarled fingers. The air is thick with the scent of pine needles crushed underfoot, mingling with the faint trace of incense that seems to linger in this place—a place where the heavens and the earth draw closer together.

The sun rises slowly over the hills, casting a warm, golden light that cuts through the cool morning mist. Ahead, a small wooden chapel stands, its roof weathered by years of rain and snow, its cross silhouetted against the brightening sky. It is here, on this remote hilltop in Northern California, that pilgrims have come for years, seeking something ancient, something hidden, something true. Today, they gather again—some for the first time, others for the hundredth—drawn by an invisible thread that pulls at their hearts and brings them to this holy ground.

LIGHT JOURNEY

This book is about those who make such journeys—journeys that are both physical and spiritual, that cross not only landscapes but centuries, that reach beyond the borders of time and place into the very heart of faith. It is about the seekers, the sinners, the saints, and all who have found themselves on the narrow path that leads toward the light of Orthodoxy in America. It is about discovering the ancient faith in a world that feels increasingly fragmented, finding something whole and beautiful amidst the noise and chaos of modern life.

Imagine walking through the doors of a small, unassuming church in a city where no one seems to notice. Inside, the flicker of candles casts a soft glow on faces filled with reverence and hope. The scent of incense curls through the air, mingling with the low hum of the choir singing hymns that have been sung for centuries. A baby is being baptized, her tiny body dipped into the water three times, her cries rising above the soft prayers of the priest. In that moment, the world outside falls away, and what remains is the timeless rhythm of grace, a connection to something far older and deeper than the concrete streets and glass towers that surround it.

This is the heart of Orthodoxy—an unbroken chain stretching back to the apostles, through the desert fathers and the martyrs, through the saints who gave their lives to keep the flame of faith alive. And now, here in America, it finds new expression, new life, in unexpected places. From the bustling streets of New York to the quiet forests of California, from the plains of Alaska to the deserts of Arizona, Orthodoxy has taken root in this land, growing in ways no one could have predicted.

Introduction

This book is a modern pilgrimage through those places and stories. It begins with Fort Ross, where Russian missionaries planted the seeds of Orthodoxy on American soil over two hundred years ago, and it follows the paths of those early saints who brought the faith to this new world.

But the journey does not stop there. It moves into the present, into the lives of those who carry on this ancient faith today—the monks who left everything behind to pray in the desert of Arizona, the priests who serve in small parishes, the laypeople who find themselves unexpectedly drawn to this strange and beautiful way of life. It is about Father Seraphim Rose, who searched for truth in the wilderness and became a bridge to the ancient Church for so many seekers. It is about Brother Jose Muñoz, who guarded a miraculous icon with his life and became a martyr of love. It is about Elder Ephraim, who brought the monastic life of Mount Athos to North America, building spiritual havens in the most unlikely places.

And it is about you, the reader, wherever you are on your own journey. Maybe you are searching for something deeper, something real in a world that seems to offer nothing but illusions. Maybe you have heard of Orthodoxy and wondered what it is, or perhaps you have already taken the first steps on this path and want to know more. This book is for you, to accompany you on your way, to show you the stories of others who have walked this path, and to invite you to see the beauty of this faith with your own eyes.

You will meet people who were born into this faith, whose grandparents and great-grandparents crossed oceans to bring Orthodoxy to America. You will meet those who discovered it later in life, coming from every background imaginable, finding in Orthodoxy something they had been searching for all along. You will hear stories of miracles, of healings, of lives transformed by grace in ways that defy explanation. You will see the faith alive in the cities, in the countryside, in monasteries and small mission churches, in cathedrals, and in simple homes where families gather to pray.

This is a pilgrimage that invites you to step into the unknown, to walk the narrow path where saints have walked, to find the ancient faith in a new world. It is a journey of discovery, of wonder, of finding God not only in the places we expect but in the places we least expect. It is a journey that is at once deeply personal and universal, for it touches on the most profound questions of life: Who am I? Why am I here? Where am I going?

So, come with me. Come with all those who have come before, and all those who will come after. Let us walk together into the mystery, into the light, into the ancient faith that is as alive today as it ever was. Let us begin this modern pilgrimage and see where it takes us.

The road is long, but the way is open. The journey has only just begun.

The Iveron Icon
of the Mother of God

The fiery sun had dipped behind the craggy mountains near Nicea, casting long shadows across the home of a devout widow. Her modest house sat nestled on the outskirts of the city, but even here, danger loomed. It was the ninth-century reign of Emperor Theophilus, and the storm of iconoclasm raged through the Byzantine Empire. Soldiers marched with orders to seize and destroy all holy images. In their zeal, they scoured every village, every home, searching for the icons hidden by the faithful.

Inside the widow's home, a sacred image of the Mother of God—an ancient icon passed down through generations—stood tucked away in a corner. She had prayed fervently before it for years, trusting in the protection of the Theotokos. But now, as the sound of approaching soldiers echoed through the streets, her heart raced with fear.

A knock at the door. Then a crash as soldiers stormed in, eyes wild with fanaticism. One of them—a hulking man with a sneer etched on his face—spotted the icon. Without a word, he pulled a spear from his belt and thrust it into the face of the Theotokos.

Blood flowed. Real blood, trickling from the wound, bright red and unmistakable.

The soldiers froze. Their bravado shattered by the impossible sight, they stumbled back, eyes wide in terror. Murmuring curses, they fled into the night, leaving the widow trembling before the miracle she had just witnessed.

As the night deepened, the widow and her son knelt before the icon, their prayers mingling with tears of awe and desperation. They knew the soldiers would return, likely with reinforcements. The widow and her son needed to save the icon. Under the cover of darkness, they made their way to the sea, the holy image wrapped carefully in cloth.

At the shore, the widow spoke softly, her voice trembling but resolute. "Mother of God, protect this icon as you have protected me. Let it find safe harbor."

With a final prayer, she cast the icon upon the waves. It didn't sink. Instead, it stood upright, gliding across the sea as if guided by an unseen hand, moving westward, farther and farther from the shore.

Far away, on the Holy Mountain of Athos, monks of the Iveron Monastery gathered to pray. It was a quiet evening, the kind that soaked the soul in peace. But as the sun set, something extraordinary caught their eyes. A fiery pillar rose from the sea, stretching from the water to the heavens, burning brighter than the sun itself.

The Iveron Icon of the Mother of God

For days, the monks watched this mysterious light. What was it? A divine sign? The hand of God reaching down to earth? Finally, they could bear the suspense no longer. A group of monks descended to the shoreline. There, floating serenely on the water, was the icon of the Mother of God, untouched by the waves, gleaming with an otherworldly radiance.

As they approached, the icon seemed to withdraw, drifting farther out to sea. The monks tried and tried again to retrieve it, but each time they neared, the icon would move just beyond their reach.

That night, as they gathered to seek guidance, a voice rang out—a vision, a revelation. The Mother of God herself appeared to a Georgian monk named Gabriel, a humble ascetic who lived among them. "Enter the sea," she said to him, her voice tender yet commanding. "Walk upon the waves, and you shall bear my icon to safety."

The monks found Gabriel the next morning, quiet in his cell, his face aglow with the peace of one who has heard the voice of heaven. Together, they led him to the shore, their chants rising to the heavens. The sea breeze carried the sweet smell of incense as Gabriel, barefoot and unafraid, stepped onto the water.

He did not sink.

Step by step, he walked upon the waves as though upon dry land. The icon waited for him, and when he reached it, Gabriel lifted it into his arms, feeling the weight of holiness settle on his soul.

Triumphant, Gabriel carried the icon back to the monastery, where the monks greeted it with hymns of thanksgiving. They

Panagia Portaitissa

placed it in the sanctuary, vowing to guard this divine treasure with their lives.

But the Theotokos had other plans.

The next morning, the icon was gone. Panic rippled through the monastery until a monk discovered the image—hanging above the gates of the monastery. The monks returned the icon to its place of honor in the church, but the following morning, it had moved again. And again. Each time, they found it above the gates.

Finally, the Mother of God appeared once more to Gabriel. "Do not seek to hide me away," she told him. "For I shall guard this monastery. I will protect you all, both now and in the age to come."

From that moment on, the icon remained above the monastery gate, watching over the monks. It became known as

The Iveron Icon of the Mother of God

Portaitissa, the Gate-Keeper, a guardian of the Holy Mountain. The monks of Iveron rejoiced, for the icon was not just a symbol—it was a living promise of the Theotokos's protection and grace.

Centuries passed again, and the fame of the Iveron icon spread far and wide.

In 1989, a replica of the wonder-working icon was sent to Tbilisi, Georgia, a gift from the monks of Mount Athos to the faithful of that ancient Christian land. But this replica was more than just a painting. It was a living conduit of divine grace, infused with the same power that had guided the original icon across the seas centuries before.

And yet, the original icon remained at Iveron, silently standing guard over the monastery, just as the Mother of God had promised.

But there was another chapter yet to be written—a chapter that would unfold with the arrival of a humble man named Brother Jose Muñoz in the closing years of the twentieth century. Unknown to him, the Iveron icon would soon cross another ocean, not on waves but through the prayers and devotion of those who sought the protection of the Theotokos in a world descending into chaos. The story would stretch from the Holy Mountain to the distant shores of Montreal, where the miraculous myrrh would begin to flow once more.

But for now, on that quiet night on Mount Athos, the icon stood, waiting. A guardian, a promise, and a miracle yet to come.

The Night of Souls

October 31, 1997—California State Prison

The sound of steel doors clanging shut echoed through the cold, sterile corridors, signaling the finality of my fate. It was a night of reckoning, the culmination of years of spiraling out of control—addiction, crime, and despair. As I stood before the judge, the words "guilty" and "two years in state prison" reverberated in my mind, a verdict that seemed both inevitable and surreal. The weight of it all pressed down on me as I was led away in shackles, the sound of my chains mingling with the distant hum of the prison's harsh fluorescent lights.

But this night was not just about my fall. Across the world, in a dimly lit room in Athens, Greece, another drama was unfolding—a drama that would shake the Orthodox world to its core. Brother Jose Muñoz, the guardian of the miraculous myrrh-streaming Iveron icon of Montreal, was brutally murdered. As his blood was spilled, the icon—an earthly vessel of divine grace—was stolen, its fate unknown.

These two events—my conviction and the violent theft—seemed disconnected, but they were tied together in the tapestry of divine providence. As I descended into the darkness of my cell, Brother Jose was rising into the eternal light, martyred for his devotion to the Mother of God. The same night I was sentenced to imprisonment was the night Orthodoxy lost one of its most sacred treasures.

That night, October 31, 1997, was not just a turning point in my life; it was the first day of my continuing recovery. From that day forward, I have been clean and sober, a fact that still amazes me every time I reflect on the journey I've taken. The chaos of my past was finally yielding to the possibility of a new beginning, a new life. And yet, in the quiet of my prison cell, little did I know that our fates had somehow intertwined on that fateful night.

The Journey into Darkness

My journey to this moment was one of both physical and spiritual warfare. Raised under the specter of the Cold War, I followed in my father's footsteps by enlisting in the army, ready to defend my country from the looming threat of godless communism. I was trained to fight, to protect, and to kill if necessary—all in the name of something greater than myself. I worked behind the scenes, where I could see Cheyenne Mountain and the NORAD complex outside my barracks window, a constant reminder of the threat of World War III and the possibility of incoming Soviet ballistic missile strikes. But when the Cold War ended, the battles didn't. They simply moved inward, becoming wars of the soul.

After my honorable discharge, I returned to California a different man—broken, haunted, and deeply wounded. The battlefield had shifted from the behind-the-scenes logistics of the geopolitical information war and moral conflict to the inner landscapes of addiction and despair. I sought refuge in heroin, in the numbness that dulled the pain, but found only emptiness. Homeless and lost, I spiraled deeper into a world of crime and darkness, each act of theft and deceit another link in the chain that bound me.

The First Descent

Soon after my discharge from the army, I was caught shoplifting in a department store. The act was a pathetic attempt to fill the void, to maintain the addiction that had become my master. As I slipped those ties and that belt beneath my shirt, I felt the eyes on me, the cold, penetrating gaze of unseen watchers. Paranoia? Maybe. But there was something else, something more. A cosmic irony, perhaps, as I was being watched not only by security cameras but by the eyes of the soul, the eyes that saw the deeper truth of who I had become.

When the guards tackled me, when they cuffed my hands and dragged me away, I felt not just the physical restraint but the crushing weight of my own choices, the realization that I had been caught not only by man but by God. It was a slow-motion fall, as if the universe itself were replaying my sins, each frame a stark reminder of the path I had taken.

After that incident, I was in and out of jails and rehabs, jumping from one relationship to another, struggling to fill the void of my life. In spite of my intermittent addiction relapses and instabilities, I eventually managed to get a job as a counselor for a government welfare-to-work program, maintaining myself with methadone and marijuana. But even in this semblance of stability, I was haunted by the darkness within me, the gnawing emptiness that no substance or success could fill.

The Fourth of July and the Final Arrest

One hot Fourth of July evening, I drove to Angel Stadium in Anaheim to the Harvest Crusade, a sugar-coated millennial Christian rock concert led by superstar ex-surfer hippie Greg Laurie, pastor of one of Southern California's biggest megachurches. Harvest Christian Fellowship in Riverside, California was a spinoff from Chuck Smith's Calvary Chapel denomination, which grew out of the sixties Jesus People movement.

Christian pop stars dominated the stage. As the music reached a frenzied Christian rock crescendo, Greg Laurie culminated his emotional sermon about the wasted lives of glamorous pursuits and the value of sacrifice. The service ended with an impassioned altar call and hypnotic music urging everyone to repent and come down to the front so they could be prayed for and fill out cards with their contact information. I took comfort in the thought that I was already "saved" and didn't need to go back down to give my life to the Lord again. After all, once saved, always saved, I thought to myself as I headed back to the parking lot. Fireworks exploded over Angel Stadium, scintillating like jewels against the velvet night. Red, white, and blue explosions lit up the Fourth of July night sky above us, pop-pop-popping in the distance, fire in the heavens.

The next day, a police car pulled up behind me, red lights flashing. The officer pulled me over and searched my car, finding several ounces of marijuana and a loaded handgun. After getting out on bail and fighting the case as long as I could, I was eventually sentenced to two years in state prison. BAM! Doors slammed and I was gone.

As the darkness of doom descended, I was facing the reality of my impending death—alone, broken, and abandoned. But in that bleakness, in that moment of utter despair, there was a flicker of something else—something that would not fully reveal itself until much later. It was the light of grace, the same light that had guided the saints and martyrs, the light that would eventually guide me out of the darkness.

A Night of Miracles

As I lay there, teetering on the edge of life and death, the world continued to turn, oblivious to my suffering. But in that same night, as I faced my own mortality, Brother Jose was being ushered into eternity. His life, dedicated to the Mother of God, was violently cut short, but his death was not the end. The icon he had guarded, the icon that had poured forth myrrh in miraculous streams, was now missing, its whereabouts unknown but its power undiminished.

In the years to come, I would learn of Brother Jose's story, of the miracles associated with the icon, and of the mysterious events surrounding its disappearance. And in those stories, I would find echoes of my own journey—a journey from darkness to light, from death to life, from despair to hope.

My affinity for Brother Jose grew as I learned more about him, and I felt an inexplicable connection to his sacrifice. Brother Jose was born in Chili and descended from the ancient Spanish family of Cortes, in which the Virgin Mary was especially revered, and all the firstborns were named after Joseph the Betrothed and Protector of the Mother of God. Brother Jose was twelve years old when, walking by the Russian Orthodox church in Santiago, he was attracted by the sound of singing and went inside. There he became acquainted with Archbishop Leonty of blessed memory, and under his influence José was baptized into the Orthodox Church two years later, with his mother's consent.

As a university student, José was studying theology when Metropolitan (then Archbishop) Vitaly, on a trip to Chile, learned of the youth's monastic aspirations and invited him to Canada. José lived for about a year at Holy Transfiguration Monastery in Montreal, but he left to live on his own, while maintaining a strict monastic lifestyle to the end. A talented artist, he took a job teaching art at the University of Montreal and began studying iconography.

The Beginning of a New Path

That night, October 31, 1997, was not the end. It was the beginning—of my path to redemption, of my return to Christ, and of my discovery of the ancient faith that had been hidden from me for so long. As the steel doors of the prison clanged shut behind me, another door was opening—a door to a life I had never imagined, a life of faith, hope, and love.

And so, my story begins not in triumph, but in the ashes of defeat. But it is from these ashes that the fire of faith would be rekindled, leading me to the Orthodox Church and to a life transformed by grace.

The Night of Souls

I have since had the blessing of seeing and venerating the miraculous myrrh-streaming Hawaiian Iveron icon, which continues to bring healing grace from the Mother of God, carrying on the legacy of Brother Jose and the myrrh-streaming icon of Montreal. Each time I stand before that icon, I am reminded of the night that changed everything, the night that marked the beginning of my recovery and that brought Brother Jose into eternal light.

Fort Ross today

Fort Ross and the Seeds of Orthodoxy

The Establishment of Fort Ross

The year is 1812. The fog lies thick over the Pacific as the ships of the Russian American Company cut through the cold waters, making their way toward the rugged, untouched coastline of Northern California. The wind is brisk, filling the sails, while seabirds cry out, circling above like silent witnesses. From the deck, the men catch their first glimpse of land—a dark, mysterious silhouette emerging from the mist. Captain Ivan Kuskov stands at the helm, his eyes focused on the horizon. He feels a blend of hope and anxiety, knowing that this place, which will soon be known as Fort Ross, is where the future of Russian America will be forged.

As the ships approach Bodega Bay, the mist begins to lift, revealing a stretch of towering redwoods and rocky cliffs. The land is wild, untamed—a world apart from the frozen landscapes of Alaska, where Kuskov and his men had made their home. This is a place full of promise, yet it is also a place of deep unknowns. They know that the native Kashaya Pomo people live here and that the Spanish *to the south also claim this land. But for now, this place is theirs to claim, to settle, and to begin anew.*

Fort Ross was established as a multipurpose outpost—a trading hub, an agricultural station, a place to hunt sea otters for their valuable pelts, and a potential barrier against the northward expansion of the Spanish missions. Under Kuskov's leadership, the fort quickly took shape. A wooden palisade was constructed, enclosing barracks, workshops, and a chapel dedicated to the Holy Trinity. Here, under the sound of the waves and the shadows of ancient trees, a small but vibrant community began to emerge.

From the beginning, the Orthodox faith was at the center of life at Fort Ross. The chapel with its simple wooden cross became the heart of the settlement. The prayers and liturgies offered by the company priests were a source of spiritual nourishment for the Russian settlers, Aleut hunters, and even some of the local Kashaya Pomo who lived nearby. Orthodoxy, transplanted to this distant land, began to take root and grow in the rich soil of Northern California.

The Role of Russian Missionaries in Early California

The Russian presence at Fort Ross was not solely an economic venture; it was also a spiritual mission. Russian missionaries played a crucial role in establishing the seeds of Orthodoxy in this new land. They were men who saw their task not merely as that of explorers or settlers but as that of messengers of the Gospel, bringing the light of Christ to the indigenous peoples of North America.

Fort Ross and the Seeds of Orthodoxy

Among the first and most important of these missionaries was St. Innocent of Alaska. Though his primary mission was to the native peoples of Alaska, St. Innocent's influence reached down the Pacific coast to Fort Ross. Known for his dedication to translating the Scriptures and Orthodox services into native languages, St. Innocent was a pioneer in the concept of incarnational mission—meeting people where they were and speaking to them in their own words.

St. Innocent visited Fort Ross during one of his many journeys from Alaska, bringing with him a sense of calm authority and deep compassion. He was a man of great stature; his presence filled the room. He spoke with warmth and clarity, offering counsel to the settlers and baptizing those who sought the faith. Under his guidance, the Orthodox community at Fort Ross grew in both numbers and strength. He spoke to them about the importance of living the faith sincerely and taught them that Orthodoxy was not just a set of rituals but a way of life—a journey toward God.

The story of St. Innocent of Alaska (1797–1879) reads like an epic carved from the raw, unforgiving landscapes of the Alaskan wilderness. A priest, linguist, craftsman, naturalist, and saint, he embodied the resilience and devotion required to bring the Gospel to a land both sacred and perilous. His life and work serve as a testament to the power of faith to transform not only individuals but entire cultures. As I delve deeper into his story, I am struck by the cinematic grandeur of his mission and the enduring lessons it offers to modern readers.

Born Ivan Popov-Veniaminov in the Siberian city of Irkutsk, St. Innocent was no stranger to hardship. Yet, his faith and curiosity propelled him beyond the confines of his native Russia to the uncharted spiritual and physical wilderness of Alaska. His journey began with a calling that led him across the frozen steppes of Siberia, through the tumultuous Bering Sea, and into the heart of Native Alaskan communities. Here, amidst towering glaciers and boundless tundras, he would plant seeds of Orthodoxy that continue to bear fruit centuries later.

A Renaissance Missionary

St. Innocent's three decades in Alaska were nothing short of extraordinary. A man of immense intellect and unyielding determination, he mastered several Native Alaskan dialects and devised alphabets, grammars, and dictionaries to translate the Holy Scriptures and liturgical texts into indigenous languages. His work was not limited to linguistics; he was a skilled craftsman who built churches, furniture, and even musical instruments. He also established schools and trained local clergy, ensuring that the faith he planted would be nurtured by those it belonged to.

One of his most remarkable feats was his ability to connect with the Native Alaskan people on a profound level. He respected their traditions, listened to their stories, and sought to understand their spiritual worldview. This approach was not merely pragmatic; it was deeply rooted in his belief that Christ's message was not foreign to these communities but the fulfillment of their deepest spiritual aspirations.

The Angels of Akun

Among the many accounts of St. Innocent's missionary work, his encounter on the island of Akun stands out for its miraculous and mystical elements. In 1828, as a young priest, he traveled to this remote island, where he was greeted with unexpected festivity by the Aleuts. They had been told of his arrival by an elderly shaman, Ivan Smirennikov, who claimed to have been visited by two angelic beings for decades. These "angels," clad in white garments with rose-colored bands, had instructed him in Christian teachings and virtues, helping to sustain the faith of the community in the absence of a priest.

The account of Smirennikov's visions, detailed in St. Innocent's letters, reveals the profound interplay between the divine and the human in the missionary's work. It was not simply a matter of teaching theology or performing sacraments; it was a sacred dialogue in which the Holy Spirit was palpably present. The old shaman's story, validated by his humility and the orthodoxy of his teachings, is a reminder that God's grace often works in unexpected ways, transcending cultural and geographical boundaries.

A Life of Sacrifice and Perseverance

St. Innocent's missionary efforts were not without immense personal sacrifice. In a fourteen-month span, he traveled nearly 15,000 miles by foot, dogsled, reindeer sleigh, and kayak, enduring extreme weather and physical hardship. His willingness to face these challenges was driven by a love for his flock and an unwavering commitment to the Gospel.

Even after the tragic loss of his wife, Catherine, St. Innocent's dedication did not waver. He sent his children to Irkutsk for their education and took monastic vows, adopting the name Innocent. As a bishop and later Metropolitan of Moscow, he continued to advocate for the spiritual and material well-being of his Alaskan flock, ensuring that the light of Orthodoxy would continue to shine in the northernmost reaches of the world.

Lessons from St. Innocent for Today

The story of St. Innocent is not merely historical; it is profoundly relevant to our contemporary spiritual landscape. His ability to bridge cultures with respect and love offers a model for evangelism in an increasingly pluralistic world. His dedication to education and linguistic preservation underscores the importance of contextualizing the faith without compromising its essence.

Perhaps most striking is his humility. Despite his extraordinary achievements, St. Innocent remained acutely aware of his own limitations and the sovereignty of God's will. His reluctance to meet the "angels" who appeared to Smirennikov, for fear of pride, exemplifies a profound spiritual wisdom that resonates deeply in an age often characterized by self-promotion.

A Legacy Carved in the Frozen Earth

As I reflect on the life of St. Innocent, I am reminded of the enduring power of faith to transform not only individuals but entire communities. His story is a cinematic tapestry

Fort Ross and the Seeds of Orthodoxy

of adventure, sacrifice, and divine grace, set against the stark beauty of Alaska's wilderness. It is a story that calls us to look beyond the confines of our own lives and embrace the boundless possibilities of God's love.

St. Innocent's legacy lives on in the Native Alaskan communities that continue to practice the Orthodox faith he so lovingly nurtured. It lives on in the churches he built, the languages he preserved, and the souls he shepherded. And it lives on in each of us who are inspired by his example to seek the sacred in the ordinary, to love without reservation, and to carry the light of Christ into the darkest corners of the world.

Decades later, the young priest Sebastian Dabovich, who would later become known as St. Sebastian of Jackson, would forge his own unique connection to Fort Ross. He was baptized on a Russian naval ship off the coast of San Francisco Bay, not far from the fort itself. Raised in the Serbian Orthodox tradition, St. Sebastian was profoundly influenced by the Russian clergy he encountered during his formative years. He would often speak of the early Russian missionaries with reverence, seeing in them a model for his own future work.

In his later years, St. Sebastian would return to Fort Ross to serve the Divine Liturgy, drawn by its historical and spiritual significance. He saw in this humble settlement the birthplace of Orthodoxy in California, a place where the faith had first been planted on these shores. His visits were marked by deep prayer and reflection, and he often spoke to others about the need to continue the missionary spirit of the early Russian settlers.

Saint Tikhon and the Blessing of Fort Ross

Another towering figure in the story of Fort Ross was St. Tikhon of Moscow, who visited California in the early twentieth century as part of his duties as Bishop of the Aleutians and North America. He was a man of vision, deeply aware of the need to preserve and expand the Orthodox faith on this continent. During his time in California, St. Tikhon visited Fort Ross, offering prayers and blessings over the land where so much had begun.

St. Tikhon saw Fort Ross as a spiritual landmark, a place that held the memory of the early Russian efforts to plant the faith in America. He spoke of the need to honor the legacy of those who had come before, who had labored in harsh conditions to establish a foothold for Orthodoxy in the New World. He emphasized the importance of preserving this site not merely as a historical artifact but as a living part of the Church's mission.

During his visit, St. Tikhon celebrated a Divine Liturgy at the chapel of Fort Ross, his voice ringing out with the ancient hymns of the Church, the words echoing off the wooden walls as if the very building were joining in prayer. It was a moment that seemed to transcend time, connecting those who stood there with the first settlers and with the saints who had walked these grounds. St. Tikhon spoke of the great spiritual potential of America, urging his listeners to see Fort Ross not as a relic of the past but as a seed of Orthodoxy's future.

His words found fertile ground. Even today, many who visit Fort Ross speak of a sense of presence, a feeling that this place is more than just an old fort; it is a holy ground, blessed by the prayers and labors of those who came before.

Saint John the Wonderworker and His Pilgrimage to Fort Ross

Decades later, in the mid-twentieth century, another saint would make his way to Fort Ross—St. John Maximovitch the Wonderworker of Shanghai and San Francisco. A man of small stature but immense spiritual power, St. John had a deep devotion to the saints who had preceded him and a keen sense of the spiritual geography of the places he visited.

St. John was known for his tireless work, traveling frequently between his diocese of San Francisco and the far reaches of the Russian diaspora. In his journeys, he made a point to visit Fort Ross, drawn by the memory of the early Russian settlers and the spirit of missionary work that had been sown there. He came not just as a bishop but as a pilgrim, eager to walk the paths of his predecessors.

On one of his visits, St. John celebrated the Divine Liturgy at the chapel of Fort Ross. Those who attended recalled the sense of awe that filled the room as he prayed, his frail hands lifting the chalice with surprising strength, his eyes closed in deep communion with God. There were stories of miracles— of healings, of people finding answers to long-held questions, of a peace that settled over the fort like a gentle mist from the Pacific.

I remember attending one of the annual Divine Liturgies at Fort Ross on the Fourth of July, when the air was filled with the scent of saltwater and wildflowers. The sun shone brightly, casting lengthy silhouettes through the trees as the clergy processed to the chapel, their vestments shimmering in the morning light. We chanted the hymns of the Church, our voices rising with the wind that swept up from the ocean below.

As I stood there, I felt a deep connection to the saints who had walked this ground before us—St. Innocent, St. Tikhon, St. Sebastian, and St. John. I felt their presence in the very air, their prayers mingling with ours, their spirits encouraging us to continue the work they had begun. It was as if the veil between heaven and earth had thinned, and we were standing on holy ground, united with the Church across time and space.

Saint Peter the Aleut

Fort Ross is also known for a connection to another saint, a young martyr whose story would spread like wildfire throughout the Orthodox community. Saint Peter the Aleut, whose tale of faith and suffering would soon echo through the ages, found his place in the story of Orthodoxy's roots in America. His story is detailed in my previous book, *American Orthodox: Finding the Ancient Faith in the Modern World* and the related documentary.

For now, we stand at Fort Ross, on the edge of the vast Pacific, where the fog rolls in like a gentle shroud and the air is filled with the whispers of the past. Here, the seeds of Orthodoxy were planted, nurtured by the prayers and labors of the saints who came before us. Here, in this place where ocean meets forest, where east meets west, we continue the journey they began, carrying the light of faith into the world.

St. John the Wonderworker of San Francisco

The Miracles and Life of St. John Maximovitch

The early morning fog wrapped San Francisco in its cold embrace, drifting over the hills and down through the streets, giving the city an ethereal, almost otherworldly feel. It was here, in this city by the bay, that a humble man from a faraway land would leave an indelible mark on the hearts of countless people, both Orthodox and non-Orthodox alike. St. John Maximovitch, the Wonderworker of Shanghai and San Francisco, walked these streets, prayed in these churches, and brought the light of Christ to the people of this diverse and sprawling city.

Born in 1896 in Kharkov, Ukraine, St. John Maximovitch was raised in a noble family with deep roots in the Russian Orthodox faith. From an early age, he exhibited a profound love for prayer and the writings of the saints. His childhood was marked by a quiet devotion, a love for Christ that seemed to shine through his every action. He was an unusual child, shy

St. John of Shanghai and San Francisco

and awkward in some ways, yet filled with a fire that burned deeply within him.

His journey to sainthood began amidst the chaos and turmoil of the Russian Revolution. As a young man, he fled with his family to Yugoslavia, where he would attend seminary and later become a monk, taking the name John in honor of his relative St. John of Tobolsk, a bishop and saint whom he deeply admired. In 1926, John was ordained a priest, and by 1934, he was consecrated as a bishop and assigned to the Diocese of Shanghai, China.

It was in Shanghai, where many White Russians had fled after the revolution, that St. John first became known for his extraordinary piety and asceticism. He would walk the streets of the city at all hours of the day and night, looking for those in need. The people of Shanghai—Russians, Chinese, and others—would often see him in his ragged cassock, moving with a hurried gait, his gaze firmly fixed on the ground, muttering prayers to himself. It was said that he never slept in a bed but instead took only short naps, often while seated or kneeling, always ready to rise and pray.

St. John became known as a healer, a man whose prayers could bring about miraculous recovery from illnesses and injuries that seemed beyond human help. Parents would bring their sick children to him, and he would anoint them with oil, offer prayers, and bless them. Many would return to health, and word of St. John's miracles spread quickly throughout the Orthodox diaspora in Shanghai.

When the Communists took control of China, St. John led his flock to safety, shepherding them first to the Philippines and then to the United States. It was in San Francisco, however, that his reputation as a wonderworker truly grew. Appointed the Archbishop of the Russian Orthodox Church Outside of Russia in San Francisco, he became known not just for his miracles but also for his deep compassion, humility, and holiness.

St. John's relics rest in the Holy Virgin Cathedral on Geary Boulevard, where they draw pilgrims from all over the world. It was here that I first encountered him, face to face, in a way that I will never forget.

Personal Reflections: A Pilgrimage to St. John's Tomb

It was a chilly Sunday morning in San Francisco, the fog hanging low over the city. I had come to the Holy Virgin Cathedral with a sense of anticipation and a heart full of prayers. I had heard so much about St. John Maximovitch, the Wonderworker of San Francisco, and now I was here, standing before the place where his relics rested.

The cathedral was quiet, a few candles flickering near the front, their soft light dancing across the walls. I moved slowly, almost hesitantly, toward the tomb of St. John. As I approached, I felt a warmth radiating from the glass case that held his relics. It was as if a gentle presence surrounded him, a sense of peace that filled the air. I knelt down, my heart pounding, and whispered a prayer.

I asked St. John for his intercession, for guidance and help in finding a new job and a home. I had been struggling for months, caught in a whirlwind of uncertainty and anxiety. I felt lost, unsure of my path, and I needed a sign, a direction, something to hold onto. As I prayed, I felt a calmness settle over me, a peace that seemed to ease the tension in my heart. I stayed there for what felt like hours, whispering my prayers, feeling tears on my cheeks.

Days turned into weeks, and as I continued to seek St. John's intercession, things began to change. I was offered a job in Sacramento, an opportunity that seemed to come out of nowhere. The offer was unexpected, almost miraculous, a perfect fit for my skills and desires. Soon after, I found a home that felt as if it had been waiting for me. It was as if St. John had guided my steps, opening doors that I had not even seen before.

I returned to the Holy Virgin Cathedral to give thanks, kneeling again before the saint's relics, this time with a heart filled with gratitude. I knew that he had heard my prayers, that he had interceded on my behalf, and I felt a connection to him that I had never felt before with any saint. St. John had become a guide, a spiritual father, a friend in heaven whose prayers had changed the course of my life.

A Mentor to Father Seraphim Rose

It was not just my own life that St. John had touched. His spiritual mentorship extended to many others, including Father Seraphim Rose, one of the most beloved and controversial Orthodox figures in America today.

When Eugene Rose—who would later become Father Seraphim—first encountered Orthodoxy, he was a young man searching for truth in a world that seemed increasingly devoid of it. He had been exploring various philosophies and religious traditions, looking for something that resonated with the deepest longings of his heart. When he stepped into a Russian

Orthodox Church in San Francisco for the first time, he felt something he had never felt before—a sense of coming home.

Eugene soon came under the guidance of Archbishop John, who took a particular interest in the young man's spiritual development. Archbishop John saw in him a deep thirst for God, a hunger for truth, and he began to mentor him closely. He taught Eugene to pray, to read the lives of the saints, and to immerse himself in the teachings of the Church Fathers.

Archbishop John was not just a teacher to Eugene; he was a living example of holiness. Eugene would often speak of how deeply he was moved by the archbishop's humility, his compassion, and his unwavering dedication to his flock. He saw in St. John a man who truly lived what he preached, a man whose life was marked by a deep and abiding love for Christ.

This mentorship profoundly shaped Eugene's journey into Orthodoxy. When he decided to become a monk and eventually founded the St. Herman of Alaska Monastery in Platina, California, the teachings and example of St. John were always in his heart. Father Seraphim would often refer to St. John as his spiritual father, the one who had guided him through the early years of his Orthodox faith.

Years later, as a monk, Father Seraphim would speak of Archbishop John with great reverence. He would tell his own spiritual children about the archbishop's miracles, his prayers, and his profound love for the people of God. Even in the remote mountains of Northern California, where the St. Herman of Alaska Monastery stood, St. John's presence could be felt. His prayers seemed to reach across time and space, guiding and protecting those who sought his intercession.

Modern Relevance of St. John's Life and Miracles

St. John's life and miracles continue to resonate in the hearts of the faithful, both in America and around the world. His love for the poor, the sick, and the suffering was not confined to his own time; it extends to all who call upon him today. He is a saint for our times, a wonderworker whose life reminds us that holiness is not an abstract concept but a living reality, accessible to all who seek it.

Many who come to venerate his relics at the Holy Virgin Cathedral speak of a sense of peace, a sense that they are standing in the presence of something divine. They come with prayers and petitions, asking for healing, for guidance, for comfort in times of distress. And time and again, they leave with their prayers answered, their hearts lifted, and their spirits renewed.

I have heard countless stories from others who, like me, have experienced St. John's intercession in their lives. A young mother who prayed for her child's recovery from a severe illness, only to see her child healed almost overnight. An elderly man who asked for help with a financial crisis and found unexpected assistance that resolved his problems. A student who prayed for clarity and purpose and found a new direction in life.

But St. John's relevance is not just in his miracles; it is in the example of his life. In a world that often feels chaotic, divided, and filled with suffering, St. John shows us what it means to live a life of love, humility, and service to others. He teaches us that the way to God is not through grand gestures or lofty ideals but through simple, everyday acts of kindness and compassion.

His mentorship of Father Seraphim Rose is a powerful testament to this truth. Father Seraphim, who would go on to become one of the most beloved Orthodox writers and teachers in America, often spoke of how St. John taught him to find God in the ordinary, to see the divine in the mundane, to live a life that was wholly dedicated to Christ.

St. John continues to teach us today, not just through his words but through his example. He shows us that it is possible to live a holy life, even amid the most challenging circumstances. He reminds us that every moment is an opportunity for prayer, every encounter is a chance to show love, and every hardship is a path to deeper communion with God.

A Saint for All Times

As I write these words, I think back to my own journey, to that moment when I knelt before St. John's tomb and asked for his help. I think of the peace that filled my heart, the way my life began to change, the sense that I was not alone, that I was being guided by a hand unseen. I know that St. John's prayers were with me then, and I feel them still.

St. John Maximovitch is more than a figure of the past; he is a living presence, a beacon of light in a world that often feels dark and confusing. His miracles, his prayers, his example of love and humility—these are gifts he continues to offer to us, gifts that can guide us on our own journeys of faith.

For those of us who seek a deeper connection to God, who long to live lives that are rich in meaning and purpose, St. John is a companion, a guide, a friend who walks with us every step of the way. His life shows us that sainthood is not about perfection but about striving, not about grandeur but about grace, not about achieving but about receiving the love of God and sharing it with the world.

In every prayer, in every act of kindness, in every moment of grace, St. John the Wonderworker is there, reminding us that the kingdom of God is within us, that the path to holiness is open to all, and that the miracles of faith are all around us, waiting to be discovered.

Holy Father John, pray to God for us.

St. Sava Serbian Orthodox Church in Jackson, California

St. Sebastian of Jackson

THE AMERICAN MISSIONARY

The Life and Work of St. Sebastian Dabovich

The waves of the Pacific rolled gently against the side of the Russian Imperial Naval ship, anchored off the fog-shrouded coast of San Francisco. The early morning mist clung to the water, swirling around the vessel like a veil, and the air was permeated with the salty scent of the sea. On the deck of the ship, a young boy named Jovan Dabovich stood, his eyes wide with wonder and anticipation. Despite the chill in the air, he felt a deep warmth within, knowing that a sacred moment was about to unfold.

Surrounded by sailors and officers, an Orthodox priest stood solemnly, his vestments billowing slightly in the ocean breeze, his hands lifted in prayer. The priest's voice carried over the sound of the waves, invoking the Holy Trinity as he began the sacrament of baptism. Jovan, who would one day be known as St. Sebastian of Jackson, was gently immersed three times in the waters of baptism, each immersion accompanied by the priest's invocation of the Father, the Son, and the Holy Spirit. As Jovan emerged from the *water, a serene light seemed to illuminate his young face, his spirit forever marked by the sacredness of this moment.*

This baptism aboard the Russian naval ship was more than a mere ritual; it was the beginning of a profound spiritual journey. Jovan Dabovich, later known as Sebastian, was born in San Francisco in 1863 to Serbian immigrant parents seeking a new life in America. From a young age, he was deeply rooted in the traditions of the Orthodox Church, nurtured by the devout faith of his mother and father. The baptism on the deck of that Russian ship planted a seed in his heart—a seed that would grow into an unshakable love for Christ and His Church, guiding him to become one of the most significant missionaries of Orthodoxy in America.

A Need for a Shepherd: The Serbian Immigrants in Northern California

During the mid-nineteenth century, as the California Gold Rush drew prospectors and adventurers from all over the world, many Serbian immigrants found their way to Northern California. They came seeking fortunes in the gold mines, hoping to carve out a new life in the harsh foothills of the Sierra Nevada. Towns like Jackson became home to these hopeful immigrants, who worked tirelessly, digging and panning for gold, their hands stained with earth and sweat. Amid their toil, they felt a deep yearning for something beyond material wealth—a spiritual connection to their homeland, the familiar rhythms of their faith.

Separated from the churches of their homeland, they longed for a priest to shepherd them, to celebrate the Divine Liturgy, to baptize their children, marry their young, and bury their dead with the rites of the Orthodox Church. It was a deep yearning for a spiritual anchor, a need that would soon be met by a young priest named Father Sebastian Dabovich.

The Establishment of St. Sava Serbian Orthodox Church

As Father Sebastian began his ministry in America, he felt a calling to serve his people in California. He saw the need for a spiritual center where the Serbian community could gather, worship, and maintain their cultural and religious heritage. With great effort and dedication, he founded St. Sava Serbian Orthodox Church in Jackson, California—the first Serbian Orthodox church in the Western Hemisphere and the second oldest Orthodox Christian parish in California.

The church itself is a jewel of Orthodox architecture, standing quietly amidst the rolling hills of Jackson. Built in the late nineteenth century, St. Sava Church is constructed in a style that combines the simplicity of pioneer American structures with the distinctive elements of Serbian ecclesiastical design. The wooden frame building is painted a crisp white, standing in stark contrast to the surrounding landscape. Its modest bell tower rises toward the sky, crowned with a golden Orthodox cross, a beacon of faith in the heart of the California countryside.

The interior of St. Sava Church is warm and intimate, filled with the rich scent of beeswax candles and incense. The walls are adorned with icons of Christ, the Theotokos, and various saints, painted in the traditional Byzantine style, their vibrant colors standing out against the plain white walls. The wooden pews, worn smooth by generations of worshippers, face the iconostasis—a simple yet elegant screen that separates the nave from the sanctuary. The iconostasis is adorned with images of Christ, the Mother of God, and the saints, each icon seeming to glow with an inner light.

The church's beauty is in its simplicity and the palpable sense of history that fills the space. The wooden beams overhead creak slightly with the passage of time, and the floorboards whisper underfoot, as if carrying the prayers of countless faithful souls who have stood there over the years. It is a place that feels alive, infused with the spirit of those who built it, worshiped in it, and kept the faith alive within its walls.

A Personal Pilgrimage to St. Sava Church

I have visited St. Sava Serbian Orthodox Church in Jackson many times, especially on their feast days, and each visit feels like a pilgrimage, a return to a sacred place that holds the essence of the past while pointing to the future.

On a crisp morning, I found myself once again standing outside the church, the sun stretching its light across the ground and the bells ringing out over the hills. I could feel the spirit of St. Sebastian in that place, the quiet strength of his presence, his dedication to the faith that had brought him to this remote corner of California.

Inside, the congregation had gathered for the Divine Liturgy. The faithful filled the pews, their voices lifting in song, the ancient hymns resonating through the small wooden structure. I watched as Father Marko, the parish priest, prepared for the service, his movements deliberate and reverent, embodying the spirit of St. Sebastian. Father Marko, featured in the documentary *American Orthodox*, had spoken with me before about the legacy of St. Sebastian. "He was a shepherd for all people," he said. "He cared deeply for every soul, not just for Serbs, but for anyone who came seeking the truth of God."

On this visit, I found myself drawn to the relics of St. Sebastian, which are enshrined in the church. They are housed in a simple reliquary, placed near the iconostasis, where the faithful can come forward to venerate and seek his intercession. As I knelt before the relics, I felt a deep sense of peace, a connection to the countless others who had knelt there, who had sought the prayers of this holy man.

I could feel the history of the place around me—the stories of those who had come before, the Serbian immigrants who had built this church with their hands and their hearts, who had kept the faith alive in this distant land. I thought of the countless times they must have gathered here, in moments of joy and sorrow, their prayers mingling with the smoke of incense rising to the heavens.

St. Sebastian's Broader Missionary Work and Legacy

St. Sebastian's work in Jackson was just one part of his broader mission to bring the Orthodox faith to America. He traveled widely, serving communities across the United States, from Alaska to New York, from Chicago to Los Angeles. He established parishes, preached the gospel, and brought the sacraments to the faithful, no matter where they were. His dedication to the faith and his love for the people he served knew no bounds.

He was a man of vision, seeing the potential for Orthodoxy in America long before others did. He understood that the future of the faith lay in reaching out to all people, regardless of their background or ethnicity. He worked tirelessly to establish a truly American Orthodoxy, one that honored the traditions of the past while embracing the realities of the present.

Father Sebastian was also a prolific writer and translator. He authored numerous books, pamphlets, and articles in multiple languages, aiming to make the Orthodox faith accessible to as many people as possible. His writings reflect his deep understanding of the faith, his pastoral heart, and his desire to share the love of Christ with all.

A Continuing Legacy in Jackson and Beyond

Today, St. Sava Serbian Orthodox Church stands as a testament to the enduring faith of the Serbian community in America and the pioneering work of St. Sebastian Dabovich. It remains a place of pilgrimage, prayer, and spiritual renewal.

Father Marko, who serves the church with humility and dedication, embodies the spirit of St. Sebastian in his ministry. He leads the community with a gentle hand and a warm heart, reminding them always of the importance of faith, of love, of remaining connected to their roots while embracing the future.

St. Sebastian's life and work continue to inspire those who visit St. Sava Church. His relics rest in peace, but his spirit is alive, guiding, praying, and interceding for all who seek his

St. Sebastian of Jackson

help. Those who come to this quiet place in Jackson find more than a historical site; they find a living testament to the power of faith, the strength of community, and the enduring love of God.

The Spiritual Fathers and Mothers of America

SAINTS RAPHAEL, ALEXIS TOTH, JOHN KOCHUROV OF CHICAGO, AND OLGA MICHAEL OF ALASKA

The Battle of Pacific Street

The streets of Brooklyn were tense on the night of September 19, 1905. Two groups of armed men, Syrian Orthodox Christians and Maronites, stood facing each other, their eyes filled with suspicion and animosity. The quiet of Pacific Street was shattered by the sudden clamor of a dozen voices, the glint of moonlight on metal as weapons were drawn.

In the middle of the chaos stood St. Raphael Hawaweeny, the beloved bishop of the Orthodox community, his eyes wide with concern, his heart heavy with the burden of peace. A pistol shot rang out, followed by a burst of gunfire. St. Raphael, flanked by his parishioners, had come here hoping to talk down the violence, to sit down with his adversary, Naoum Mokarzel, and end the hostilities between the Orthodox and Maronite factions. Instead, he found himself caught in a scene that seemed to come from a war zone.

As the bishop moved through the crowd, attempting to calm his people, another shot rang out, grazing the air near his head. St. Raphael knew that he had to act quickly or risk losing lives. He managed to shield himself with his cloak, his body a barrier between the two warring groups. His goal was clear: to make peace, even if it meant risking his own life. Despite his efforts, the violence escalated. The ensuing gunfight, later dubbed the Battle of Pacific Street, was brief but intense. Though no one was killed, the incident would forever mark the history of Orthodox Christianity in America and cement St. Raphael's legacy as a spiritual leader who sought peace in the face of conflict.

St. Raphael of Brooklyn: A Man of Peace Amidst Conflict

St. Raphael Hawaweeny was known for his deep commitment to peace, yet he was also a man who understood the complexities of his time. Born in Damascus in 1860, Raphael's journey to becoming the first Orthodox bishop consecrated on American soil was filled with moments of faith, struggle, and leadership. The Battle of Pacific Street exemplified his tireless work to keep the community united despite the challenges they faced from both external forces and internal divisions.

Saint Raphael's role during the battle was crucial. It was nearly midnight when the confrontation began. The Orthodox were on their way to visit an assault victim, Abousamra, but tensions quickly escalated when they encountered Mokarzel's group. St. Raphael, who believed he could mediate and stop the violence by engaging with Mokarzel directly, found himself in the center of a conflict that seemed to have no end. Some accounts suggest that a tense meeting preceded the violence, while others claim the fight broke out immediately. Regardless, the resulting gunfight, with over twenty shots fired, ended with several injuries and arrests, including that of St. Raphael.

The press portrayed the event differently, with some sources accusing St. Raphael of brandishing a gun, an allegation he vehemently denied. Despite his arrest and the challenges he faced, St. Raphael remained undeterred in his mission to serve as a shepherd to his people. His work extended far beyond the conflict on Pacific Street; he went on to consecrate many churches and ordain countless priests, ensuring the growth of Orthodoxy across North America. For his steadfast dedication, he was canonized in 2000, remembered as a beacon of peace and unity.

Saint Alexis Toth: Defender of Orthodoxy

Saint Alexis Toth, another critical figure in the spread of Orthodoxy in America, faced his own set of challenges. Born in 1853 in the Austro-Hungarian Empire, Alexis came to America to serve as a Greek Catholic priest in Minneapolis. However, upon his arrival in 1889, he was met with hostility from the local Roman Catholic bishop, who refused to recognize his ordination because of his married status. This confrontation marked the beginning of Alexis's long struggle to find a spiritual home for himself and his flock.

Disillusioned by the rejection from the Roman Catholic hierarchy, Alexis found refuge within the Orthodox Church. He met with Bishop Vladimir of San Francisco, who welcomed him and his parishioners into the Orthodox faith. Over time, Alexis became a fervent advocate for Orthodoxy, leading many Eastern Rite Catholics who felt alienated by the Roman Church to join the Orthodox Church. Through his missionary work, he established numerous parishes and inspired countless conversions, making him a vital figure in the history of American Orthodoxy. He was canonized in 1994 as a saint who defended the true faith with courage and conviction.

Saint John Kochurov of Chicago: Missionary of the New World

Saint John Kochurov's story begins in Russia, where he was born in 1871. His missionary journey brought him to Chicago in 1895, where he immediately set about building what would become Holy Trinity Cathedral, a landmark of Orthodox Christianity in the Midwest. He dedicated himself to serving the diverse immigrant community, translating liturgical services into both English and modern Russian, fostering unity among Orthodox Christians from different backgrounds.

His commitment to his mission was evident in his pastoral care, his dedication to education, and his tireless efforts to build up the Church. However, his life took a tragic turn with the Russian Revolution. Returning to Russia in 1916, he became a martyr, executed by Bolshevik forces in 1917. Despite his death, his impact on American Orthodoxy remains profound, particularly his example of missionary zeal and dedication to the faith. He was canonized in 1994, and his story continues to inspire new generations of Orthodox Christians.

Saint Olga Michael of Alaska: A Helper in Restoring the Work of God's Hands

The snow fell steadily on the village of Kwethluk, Alaska, covering the ground in a soft blanket of white. Inside a small wooden house, Matushka Olga Michael sat by the fire, her hands busy with needlework, her eyes filled with a quiet wisdom. She was known throughout the village, and indeed across Alaska, as a woman of deep faith, compassion, and a healing touch. Her life had been marked by humility and service, not only to her family and church but also to the countless people who came to her for comfort and guidance.

Matushka Olga, the wife of Archpriest Nikolai Michael, was not physically imposing but was known for her deep spiritual presence. She raised eight children and spent much of her time serving others in her village and beyond. After her passing in 1979, her sanctity began to be revealed through countless stories of miraculous healings, particularly for women suffering from trauma and abuse.

She became known for her special intercessions, especially for victims of abuse, and her grave in Kwethluk became a pilgrimage site. Pilgrims reported feelings of peace, healing, and profound spiritual presence at her resting place. The weather at her funeral, uncharacteristically mild for November in Alaska, seemed to reflect the natural world's recognition of her holiness. Birds, long since flown south for the winter, appeared during her procession, and the ground softened to allow her burial. These events contributed to the growing recognition of her sanctity.

Adding to the stories already known, accounts emerged of St. Olga appearing to people in visions, providing comfort and healing. One woman, tormented by childhood abuse, saw St. Olga in a vision guiding her through a process of emotional and spiritual healing. Another experienced St. Olga's comforting presence in a dream, providing reassurance and solace in the face of grave illness. Over time, these stories have spread beyond Alaska, drawing attention from Orthodox Christians worldwide. On November 9, 2023, the Holy Synod of the Orthodox Church in America announced St. Olga's formal canonization, with her feast day set for October 27. Celebrations of her glorification were conducted in her hometown of Kwethluck as well as in Anchorage, Alaska in 2025.

Her miracles are particularly striking because of their gentleness and their power to heal deep emotional wounds. Saint Olga has been called upon to comfort those who have experienced abuse, trauma, and suffering, and her intercessions have brought peace to many lives. She is remembered as a humble servant of God, a woman whose simple yet profound life of faith continues to touch the hearts of those who hear her story.

Conclusion:
The Spiritual Fathers and Mothers of America

The lives of Saints Raphael Hawaweeny, Alexis Toth, John Kochurov, and Olga Michael form a rich tapestry of faith, sacrifice, and service that continues to inspire Orthodox Christians in America today. Through their unique stories, these saints have each contributed to the expansion and deepening of Orthodoxy across North America. They remind us of the diverse ways in which the faith has taken root and grown, providing spiritual guidance, hope, and healing to countless individuals.

Their legacies continue to resonate, encouraging modern believers to follow their example of unwavering faith and service to God and neighbor. As we look to their lives, we see a reflection of the ongoing journey of Orthodoxy in America—a journey that is marked by both challenges and profound grace, a journey that calls each of us to deepen our commitment to living a life of faith, just as they did.

The tomb of Fr. Seraphim Rose, St. Herman's Monastery, Platina, California

Father Seraphim Rose

THE QUIET FIRE

A Life of Seeking

The streets of San Francisco were alive with noise and movement, a vibrant mix of cultures and ideas converging under the foggy embrace of the city. It was the late 1950s, a time when the world seemed to be shifting beneath everyone's feet, and Eugene Rose, a young man in his twenties, was caught in the middle of it all. He walked with purpose through Chinatown, past the neon-lit windows of jazz clubs and bookstores, his head full of questions. The city was a cacophony of life, but inside, Eugene felt a quiet emptiness, a void that no philosophy, no religion, no worldly pursuit seemed to fill.

I understand that emptiness. I've felt that same restless yearning, the unquenchable thirst for truth that drives a person to search through the great spiritual traditions of the world. Like Eugene, I was drawn to Eastern philosophies, finding some solace in their teachings but never the sense of wholeness I sought. I read the texts, practiced the meditations, and listened to the teachers, always hoping to find that elusive peace. And, like Eugene, I found myself turning toward Orthodoxy almost by accident, feeling drawn to a faith I barely understood but sensed was profoundly true.

Eugene was a seeker, much as I was. Raised in a conventional Protestant home, he had spent years exploring various ancient philosophies and religions, from Buddhism to Taoism, diving into their sacred texts and practices with a fierce determination to uncover the truth. Yet each encounter left him thirsting for more, each answer only deepening the questions that seemed to have no end.

One day, a friend suggested he visit a Russian Orthodox church in the city, another tradition to explore on his quest. Eugene agreed, not expecting much. "When I visited an Orthodox Church, it was only to view another 'tradition,'" he would later write. However, when he stepped through the doors of the church for the first time, something happened that he had not experienced in any Buddhist or other Eastern temple. "Something in my heart said this was 'home,' that all my search was over. I didn't really know what this meant, because the service was quite strange to me and in a foreign language."

Reading these words years later, I felt an echo in my own heart. I remember stepping into an Orthodox church for the first time, surrounded by icons and ancient hymns in a language I did not know. And yet, there was something undeniably familiar, something that whispered, "This is where you belong." Eugene had felt it too, that sense of coming home to a place you had never been.

Eugene's conversion was not instantaneous, but a seed had been planted that would slowly grow and change his entire life. Nearly three years would pass from the time he first entered an Orthodox church until he came to fully embrace the faith and give his life to this Person: Jesus Christ. He was received into the Orthodox Church in February 1962, on the Sunday of the Prodigal Son. Like the son in that parable, Eugene returned to the embrace of the Father and never turned back. His old life was over; a new life had begun.

He immersed himself in the life of the Russian Orthodox Cathedral in San Francisco, where he caught the attention of the cathedral's bishop: Archbishop John Maximovitch, now venerated around the world as St. John of San Francisco. Archbishop John saw in Eugene a sincerity, a depth, and a longing for God that mirrored his own. He took Eugene under his wing, guiding him as he grew in the Orthodox faith. Eugene wrote of his mentor, "If you ask anyone who knew Archbishop John what it was that drew people to him . . . the answer is always the same: he was overflowing with love; he sacrificed himself for his fellow men out of absolutely unselfish love for God and for them."

It was through Eugene's writings on nihilism and his reflections on the ancient Fathers that I first encountered his work. I was searching for answers, feeling lost between worlds, and here was a man who had also walked this path of seeking and found his way. His words were not just intellectual musings; they were a lifeline, a call to dive deeper into the mystery of Orthodoxy.

Platina Monastery: A New Monastic Vision

The road to Platina was long and winding, snaking through the mystic hills of Northern California. Dust swirled in the wake of a pickup truck as it climbed higher into the wilderness, past scattered pines and rocky outcrops. The landscape was stark and unforgiving, but there was a strange beauty in its desolation—a sense of isolation that seemed to offer freedom from the world below. It was here, in this remote, untamed terrain, that Eugene—now Father Seraphim—and his fellow monastic, Father Herman, had chosen to plant a seed of ancient faith.

I remember my first visit to Platina, years after Father Seraphim's repose. The silence of the place struck me first—a silence that seemed to carry weight, like a thick mist hovering over the hills. The small cabin that served as the monastery was plain, almost austere, blending into the weathered landscape around it. But there was a presence here, a sense of something sacred that hung in the air. I understood why Father Seraphim had chosen this place to live out his calling.

For Father Seraphim, Platina was a refuge from the world and a beacon of light, a place where the ancient monastic traditions could be revived in the modern world. The cabin was simple—a small chapel, a few cells, a garden, and a woodstove that seemed to struggle against the biting cold. Here, Father Seraphim embraced the monastic life with a fervor that matched his earlier intellectual pursuits. He prayed, fasted, and worked, finding in this simplicity a deeper connection to God.

Yet his vision for Platina was not one of retreat but of transformation. He believed that the monastery could become a spiritual center for others, a place where people could come to find the original Christianity of the early Church Fathers. He began writing, translating ancient texts and making the wisdom of the Holy Fathers accessible to a new generation of seekers.

When I read his writings, I felt as if he were speaking directly to me—to all of us who have ever wandered, searching for something that the modern world could not provide. His words were both a challenge and an invitation, a call to look beyond the surface and find the deeper reality beneath.

Visitors began to find their way to Platina, drawn by Father Seraphim's teachings and his quiet, unassuming presence. He welcomed them with a gentle humility, listening more than he spoke, guiding them not with grand gestures or dramatic proclamations but with a simple, steady faith that burned like a quiet fire. He was not a man of spectacle, but there was something in his eyes—a calm certainty that spoke of a peace he had found, a peace he wanted to share.

For those who came, Platina became a place where heaven and earth met, where the sacred could be touched in the ordinary, where the Divine Liturgy chanted in the small chapel felt like the very song of angels.

Controversies and Contributions

But not everyone was drawn to Platina with reverence. Over time, voices of criticism began to arise, questioning Father Seraphim's teachings, his methods, his very approach to Orthodoxy. Some viewed him as a radical, a fundamentalist too eager to draw sharp lines in the sand, too insistent on the purity of tradition in a time of modernity and change. Others criticized his previous lifestyle choices and moral shortcomings prior to his dedication to the Orthodox Church.

His critiques of modern spiritual movements and ecumenism sparked debates within and beyond the Orthodox community. I read these writings with a mix of admiration and caution, recognizing both Father Seraphim's fierce commitment to Orthodoxy and the tension it created. He spoke openly against what he saw as the compromises of the age, his words sharp, his tone sometimes severe. But beneath the sharpness, there was love—a deep love for the Church and a desire to protect its truth.

To some, Father Seraphim was a spiritual father, a guide for their journey; to others, he was a monk whose fervor seemed too extreme. He never sought to be a hero, only to be faithful to what he believed. He continued his work, translating texts, writing, and teaching, his writings finding their way into the hands of many who were searching for something more.

He helped to revive monasticism in America, showing it not as a relic of the past but as a living tradition that speaks to the deep hunger of the human soul. His life was a quiet fire—one that burned steadily, without fanfare, but with a warmth that continues to draw people into its glow.

Even now, as I write these words, I feel his presence as a guiding force. His life reminds me that the path of faith is not always clear, not always easy, but always worth the journey. Father Seraphim Rose remains a figure of both inspiration and controversy, a man whose life embodied the tension between the old and the new, between the radical and the traditional, between the seeker and the settled.

He sought not to be loved, but to love deeply the God who called him to this remote hilltop, where the ancient faith continues to find its place in the modern world. And so the pilgrims still come, to walk the path he walked, to find in his writings a spark of that same quiet fire that burned within him, and to feel the presence of a man who remains, even in death, a guide for those who seek the ancient way in a new land.

September 2, 1982: Repose of Father Seraphim Rose

The morning sun rises over the golden hills of Northern California, its light spreading slowly through the dense canopy of trees that surrounds St. Herman of Alaska Monastery in Platina. The air is warm, unusual for early September, but inside the small monastery church, the atmosphere is charged with a sense of the extraordinary. For three days, Father Seraphim Rose's body has lain in state, unembalmed, in the simple wooden coffin that rests in the center of the nave. His face is serene, almost smiling, his skin soft and glowing with a golden hue. There is no sign of decay, no stiffness, only a blessed stillness that seems to defy the natural order.

The small church is filled to overflowing. Monks, pilgrims, and visitors from across the country and beyond crowd into every available space. Even the youngest children, who would normally shy away from such a sight, are drawn close, crowding around the coffin, their innocent eyes wide with wonder rather than fear. The air is thick with the fragrance of incense, mingling with the scent of fresh flowers that have been placed all around. It is more like a feast than a funeral, a solemn yet joyous celebration of a life that seems to transcend death itself.

The chant of the monks fills the space, rising and falling in waves of sound that seem to echo off the walls, filling every corner with their rich, ancient tones. The atmosphere is vibrant, alive with an inexplicable sense of grace, as if the very air has been infused with something divine. Faces that were once etched with sorrow soften, eyes that were brimming with tears now glisten with an inner light. It is as if those gathered can feel the touch of eternity breaking into this moment, bridging the gap between heaven and earth.

As the coffin is lowered into the ground, a spontaneous joy erupts from the crowd. Someone begins to sing, and soon the entire assembly joins in, their voices swelling in a triumphant chorus: "Christ is risen from the dead!" The Paschal hymn, sung at the Resurrection, fills the air, echoing off the hills and carrying their voices heavenward. The sorrow of loss is transformed into a deep and abiding joy, a joy that flows through the gathered faithful like a river of grace.

Prayers for the soul of Father Seraphim Rose continued for forty days after his repose on September 2, 1982, and pilgrimages to his grave continue every year on the anniversary of that date.

Brother Jose Muñoz

GUARDIAN OF THE MYRRH-STREAMING ICON

The Story of Brother Jose Muñoz and the Montreal Icon

Shortly after the repose of Father Seraphim Rose, on the cold, still night of November 24, 1982, in Montreal, Canada, Brother Jose Muñoz-Cortes wakes with a start, the air around him filled with a scent so sweet, so intense, that it seems almost tangible. He blinks, disoriented, his senses overwhelmed by the fragrance that fills the room. His eyes fall on the icon—a copy of the Panagia Portaitissa Icon of the Mother of God, entrusted to him on Mount Athos. The icon is shimmering, covered in a thin layer of liquid. At first, he thinks it might be oil from a votive lamp or some other source, but then he realizes—it is myrrh.

Heart pounding, Brother Jose approaches the icon, a cloth in hand, and carefully wipes it dry. Yet almost instantly, the myrrh begins to flow again, as if from an unseen source. The room is filled with its fragrance, thick and heady, almost intoxicating. For a week, the myrrh continues to stream from the icon, and the scent lingers, filling every corner of his small apartment. It is a sign, a mystery he cannot explain.

When he contacts his bishop, Vladyka Vitaly, the bishop comes, kneels before the icon, and whispers, "This is God's miracle!" The icon is brought to the cathedral, and during the liturgy, the myrrh pours out in such abundance that it drips onto the floor, soaking the wooden planks beneath it. The faithful are overcome with awe and wonder, tears streaming down their faces as they watch the miracle unfold before their eyes.

The Origin of the Iveron Icon and Brother Jose's Calling

To understand Brother Jose's role as the guardian of the Montreal Iveron icon, we must recall the story of the original Iveron icon, told earlier in this book: how it journeyed miraculously from Nicea to the Iveron Monastery on Mount Athos and became the monastery's protector.

It was a copy of this sacred icon that Brother Jose Muñoz-Cortes encountered during his pilgrimage to Mount Athos in 1982. Born in Chile, Brother Jose was an artist and iconographer who had converted to Orthodoxy from Roman Catholicism after being moved by the ancient faith's depth and mystery. His journey into Orthodoxy was one of a deep spiritual longing, a desire to find the truth that had been planted in his heart from a young age. Drawn by the call of monasticism, Brother Jose visited Mount Athos, where he felt a particular pull toward this very icon.

The monks at the Skete of the Nativity of Christ on Mount Athos, where this replica of the Iveron icon was housed, noticed his devotion. They sensed that he had been chosen for a special purpose. The monks entrusted him with the icon, telling him that it would bring blessings to many in North America. Brother Jose accepted this sacred responsibility with humility, sensing a deep spiritual connection with the Mother of God. Little did he know how true the words of the monks would prove to be.

When the icon began streaming myrrh in November of that year, Brother Jose's life took on a new mission. For fifteen years, he traveled with the icon across North America, from cathedrals in New York to small mission churches in Canada, bringing the miraculous presence of the Mother of God to countless people. Everywhere the icon went, it left a trail of grace—stories of healing, conversion, and reconciliation. Brother Jose became known as the gentle guardian of the Montreal Iveron icon, a humble servant whose only desire was to share the blessings of the Mother of God with the world.

Miracles of the Montreal Icon

But what does it mean to be a guardian of such a mystery? For fifteen years, Brother Jose faithfully cared for the icon, never seeking fame or recognition. The icon traveled far and wide—from the grand cathedrals of Europe to the humble mission churches of North America. Everywhere it went, it left a trail of grace.

There were stories of the blind who began to see, of the paralyzed who stood and walked, of those who had lost all hope finding new strength. I read these stories with fascination and wonder, not fully understanding but feeling a deep stirring within me. How could a piece of wood and paint be the source of so much grace? It defied explanation, yet the evidence was undeniable—lives were changed, bodies were healed, and souls were awakened.

One of the most compelling stories involved a woman from Quebec who had suffered for years from a debilitating illness. When she came to venerate the icon with her family, she was frail, her face marked by years of suffering, her body supported by a wheelchair. Brother Jose quietly placed the icon before her, and as she reached out to touch it, she began to weep. The scent of myrrh filled the room, and a warmth spread through her body. To the astonishment of those around her, she stood up, tears streaming down her face. "I am healed," she whispered, as if afraid to believe her own words. And indeed, she was.

I read that story years later, long after Brother Jose had been taken from this world, but it stayed with me. I had my own encounter with the miraculous power of the Mother of God, but it came much later, in 2017, when I first encountered the Hawaiian Iveron icon, another myrrh-streaming icon that seemed to continue the legacy of the Montreal icon.

The Hawaiian Iveron Icon: A New Chapter

The humid Honolulu night was still, the distant murmur of waves against the shore barely audible in the background. Inside a modest home, dimly lit by the soft glow of vigil lamps, Deacon Nectarios sat at his desk, lost in thought. The room was quiet except for the steady tick of a clock, a silence that had settled over the house like a comforting blanket. His cat, usually a creature of routine, suddenly seemed restless. The feline padded softly across the room, nose twitching, as if searching for something unseen.

Deacon Nectarios glanced up, his eyes narrowing as he watched the cat approach the small icon corner in the room, a sacred space filled with holy images and relics. The cat, who typically stayed away from the icons, now stood on its hind legs, pawing the air, clearly drawn to something. Curiosity pricked at the back of the deacon's mind. He rose from his chair and walked over, feeling a slight flutter of apprehension.

Then it hit him—a fragrance so overpowering that he stopped in his tracks. It was the scent of roses, thick and intoxicating, like walking through a garden in full bloom. For a moment, he stood still, breath caught in his throat. It was unlike anything he had ever experienced, a fragrance that seemed to fill the entire room, coming from nowhere and everywhere at once.

Deacon Nectarios crossed himself, whispering the Jesus Prayer, his heart racing. He approached the icons, scanning them one by one. Then he saw it: the small, mounted reproduction of the Iveron icon of the Mother of God, a gift from his parish priest, Father Anatole, years before. He reached out to touch it, and as his fingers brushed the surface, he felt it—wetness, a fragrant oil. Myrrh. He stared at his hand, glistening with the golden liquid, and a chill ran down his spine.

"Anna!" he called out to his wife, his voice trembling. She hurried into the room, and as she approached, her eyes widened. "Did you spill something?" he asked, though he knew the answer. She shook her head, equally stunned. The icon was wet, but the room was dry. And the scent—it was growing stronger, filling the air with a heavenly aroma. They both stood there, caught in a moment of disbelief and awe, aware that something miraculous was unfolding before them.

That night, Deacon Nectarios could barely sleep. The fragrance of roses lingered in his mind like a dream that wouldn't fade. He decided to consult Father Anatole. At the church, the priest listened carefully, then nodded. "Bring the icon here," he said simply. By Wednesday, October 10, Deacon Nectarios and his wife brought the icon to the church and placed it in the center of the nave. As Father Anatole began chanting the Akathist Hymn to the Iveron Icon, the air filled with the scent of roses. The congregation, sensing something extraordinary, watched as the icon seemed to glisten, droplets of myrrh forming on the surface.

After the service, Father Anatole inspected the icon closely, wiping it with cotton. "This is pure myrrh," he said, his voice filled with wonder. The room was alive with a sweet fragrance, and the faithful gathered around, some weeping, others whispering prayers. It was clear that this was no ordinary event. The icon remained at the church, and in the days that followed, it continued to stream myrrh. Word spread quickly, and soon people from all over—Russians, Greeks, Serbs, Roman Catholics, Protestants—flocked to the church, drawn by the miracle unfolding in their midst.

On October 14, the Feast of the Protection of the Mother of God (Julian calendar), the icon streamed so heavily that there was enough myrrh for everyone present to be anointed. Many in the congregation wept openly, overwhelmed by the palpable grace. Deacon Nectarios stood quietly at the back of the church, watching as the faithful venerated the icon. He could feel the presence of the Mother of God in a way he had never felt it before—close, comforting, and profoundly real.

In June of 2008, the Hawaiian myrrh-streaming Iveron icon was officially recognized by the Russian Orthodox Church as a miraculous and holy image. Deacon Nectarios was charged with its care and given the blessing to take it on pilgrimage, much like its predecessor, the Montreal Iveron icon. And so began the journey of this humble icon, from Hawaii to the far reaches of North America and beyond.

Wherever it traveled, miracles followed—healings, conversions, reconciliations. The blind saw again; the sick were made whole; the sorrowful found peace. It was as though the Mother of God had chosen this small, quiet parish in the middle of the Pacific to remind the world that she had not abandoned them, that her intercession was still powerful, still present.

Deacon Nectarios often found himself reflecting on those first moments, the scent of roses in his home, the wonder in his wife's eyes, the fear, the joy. He knew that this was more than a sign; it was a call—a call to believe, to trust, to witness the miracles that still happen in our modern world.

And so, with humility and a sense of awe, he continued to carry the icon, letting its grace touch the lives of those who came to see it, always remembering that the Mother of God, through this simple, myrrh-streaming icon, was still reaching out to her children with love and mercy, one drop of myrrh at a time.

Fr. Nectarios and the Hawaiian myrrh-streaming Iveron icon

I first stood before the Hawaiian Iveron icon in 2017 at Holy Virgin Cathedral in San Francisco. The air was filled with the sweet scent of myrrh, and the icon seemed to glow with an inner light. As I approached, my heart was pounding, my hands trembling with anticipation. I had read so much, heard so much, but now I was here, face to face with the mystery.

I reached out to touch the icon, feeling the cool surface of the glass covering beneath my fingers, and suddenly I was overwhelmed with a sense of peace, a sense of being held by something far greater than myself. The scent of myrrh was intoxicating, filling my senses and my soul. I felt tears on my cheeks and didn't care to wipe them away. This was a place of healing, a place where heaven and earth met, where the veil between worlds seemed to thin.

I visited the icon again in Sacramento at Holy Ascension Russian Orthodox Church, where it was brought to bless the faithful. Each time, I felt the same overwhelming presence of grace, a sense that I was standing on holy ground, that my own journey of seeking and struggling had brought me to this moment. I was not alone in this; many had come hoping for a touch of that divine love that had been made manifest through these icons.

And then in February 2020, just a few weeks before the world would be thrust into a global pandemic lockdown, my wife and I traveled to Hawaii for my birthday. I visited the church where the myrrh-streaming Hawaiian Iveron icon was kept when not touring, a small, unassuming place that radiated a quiet holiness. There, amidst the palm trees and the soft Pacific breeze, I felt the same sense of peace, the same presence that I had felt in San Francisco and Sacramento. It was as if the Mother of God was reminding me that she was always near, always present, even in the most unexpected places.

The Hawaiian Iveron icon continues to stream myrrh, continues to heal, to comfort, to call people to a deeper faith. It is kept in the Holy Theotokos of Iveron Russian Orthodox Church in Honolulu when not traveling, and it has become a focal point for prayer, pilgrimage, and devotion. People from all over the world come to venerate the icon, seeking healing, solace, and a connection to the divine. The icon's travels take it far and wide—across the United States, to Canada, Europe, and beyond—bringing the grace of the Mother of God to those who seek her intercession.

When the Hawaiian Myrrh-Streaming Iveron Icon visited Holy Ascension Russian Orthodox Church in Sacramento in 2018, Bishop Irenei of Sacramento shared a story that left the congregation spellbound. During the service, Fr. Nectarios Yangson delivered a heartfelt sermon, emphasizing that saints are not mere icons on a wall but living, acting intercessors in our lives today. With a palpable sense of urgency, he recounted stories of saints appearing to comfort the suffering—St. John the Forerunner seen among war-torn families, St. Seraphim of Sarov serving alongside monks in Greece. His words stirred hearts, but it was the miraculous account he shared from his own experience that pierced through the veil of disbelief and brought tears to many eyes.

Fr. Nectarios described a moment in Oxford, England, where a Romanian couple brought their severely afflicted young daughter to a small Moscow Patriarchate parish, seeking healing through the intercession of the Mother of God. The child, her body ravaged by an excruciating condition that caused her skin to blister and burn, sat silently as Bishop Irenei anointed her with the miraculous myrrh. As the myrrh touched her wounds, she let out a soul-shaking scream that silenced the room. Even Fr. Nectarios, the guardian of the icon who had witnessed countless miracles, found himself asking God the forbidden question: "Why? Why is this holy myrrh causing her pain?" The family quickly left the church, the haunting cry still lingering in the air.

The next morning, as they drove away from Oxford, Bishop Irenei received a phone call. After answering, he could only exclaim, "Glory to God! Glory to God! Glory to God!" When asked, he revealed the astounding news: the young girl had been completely healed overnight. Her parents, overcome with joy, discovered her giggling in her room, talking to "a lady." When they opened the door, they found her wounds gone, her skin restored, and her pain lifted—a miracle of the Theotokos. Through tears, Bishop Irenei reminded everyone that the saints are alive, longing to bring us closer to God, to love Him, and to love one another as He commands. It was a living testament to the reality of holiness and the boundless compassion of the Mother of God.

Countless stories of healing and miracles continue to be documented: from those who have been cured of cancer and other diseases to those who have found peace and solace in the face of despair. The Hawaiian icon, like its Montreal predecessor, is a living testament to the enduring love and mercy of the Mother of God.

A Journey of Grace and Mystery

Brother Jose's life was a testament to the quiet, humble faith that moves mountains. He never sought the limelight, never asked for recognition. He simply did what he felt called to do—to be a guardian of grace, a witness to the love of the Mother of God. And in his quiet way, he touched more lives than he could ever have imagined.

The Montreal icon still holds a place in the hearts of many, its story intertwined with Brother Jose's and, in a strange way, with mine. It was through these encounters, these moments of grace, that I began to see my own path more clearly, to understand that the darkness of my past was not the end of the story. There was more to come, more to discover, more to experience.

And so the pilgrimage continues. From Montreal to Hawaii, from San Francisco to Sacramento, the icons travel, carrying with them the grace of the Mother of God, the love of Christ, the hope of something beyond this world. Each encounter is a new chapter, each story a new revelation, each miracle a new reminder that we are never truly alone, that there is always light, even in the darkest places.

Brother Jose's life, death, and legacy continue to inspire, to challenge, and to call us all to a deeper faith—to see the unseen, to believe in the miracles that happen all around us, and to trust in the quiet, persistent love of God that guides us through every chapter of our lives.

Elder Ephraim of Arizona

THE SPIRITUAL BUILDER

Life of Elder Ephraim and His Path to America

The rocky hills of Mount Athos, shrouded in mist and bathed in the soft light of dawn, had been a sanctuary for monks for over a thousand years. It was here, among the ancient monasteries and the windswept landscape, that a young novice named Ioannis Moraitis, who would later become known as Elder Ephraim, began his journey to God. The air was thick with the scent of pine and wildflowers, the only sound the distant ringing of a bell calling the monks to prayer.

Born in 1928 in the small village of Volos, Greece, Ioannis grew up in a family of devout Orthodox Christians. From a young age, he felt a deep longing for God, a yearning that could not be satisfied by the comforts of worldly life. At the age of nineteen, he left his home and entered the Monastery of Philotheou on Mount Athos, where he became a spiritual child of the renowned Elder Joseph the Hesychast. Under Elder Joseph's guidance, Ioannis learned the spiritual discipline of hesychasm, a life devoted to ceaseless prayer, inner stillness, and the pursuit of divine love.

Renamed Ephraim upon his tonsure, the young monk quickly distinguished himself by his humility, obedience, and fervent prayer. Elder Joseph's teachings on the Jesus Prayer, asceticism, and spiritual warfare became the bedrock of his spiritual life. For years, Elder Ephraim lived in a small, simple cell, devoting himself to a life of prayer, fasting, and repentance. He embraced the Athonite tradition wholeheartedly, becoming known for his deep spirituality and his gift of discernment.

As Elder Joseph's most trusted disciple, Elder Ephraim inherited his spiritual legacy upon Elder Joseph's repose in 1959. Elder Ephraim became the abbot of the Monastery of Philotheou and later revitalized and reestablished several other monasteries on Mount Athos, including Xeropotamou, Konstamonitou, and Karakallou. His reputation as a spiritual father grew, and pilgrims from all over Greece and beyond came to seek his counsel, confess their sins, and receive his blessing.

But the elder's journey was far from over. In the early 1970s, he began to sense a new calling—one that would take him far from the holy mountain that had been his home for so many years. It was a calling to America, a land of spiritual thirst but also spiritual confusion, where Orthodox Christians were scattered, and the ancient traditions of the faith were in danger of being lost amid the noise and distractions of the modern world.

Founding St. Anthony's Monastery and Other Spiritual Centers

The desert stretched out before him, vast and seemingly empty, a landscape of sand and rock punctuated by cactus and sagebrush. It was a place of stark beauty, where the heat could be merciless and the nights were filled with the howls of coyotes. Elder Ephraim stood in silence, looking out over the land. This was Arizona, a place as far removed from Mount Athos as one could imagine, yet he felt a deep peace, a sense that this, too, was a holy place, waiting to be sanctified.

In 1995, after arriving in the United States, Elder Ephraim established the first of what would become a network of nineteen monasteries across North America: St. Anthony's Greek Orthodox Monastery in Florence, Arizona. Located in the Sonoran Desert, the site was chosen after much prayer and with the blessing of the late Archbishop Iakovos of the Greek Orthodox Archdiocese of America.

The founding of St. Anthony's Monastery was nothing short of miraculous. When Elder Ephraim and his small group of disciples arrived, they found an arid desert landscape that seemed ill-suited for a monastery. But Elder Ephraim saw something different; he saw potential for a spiritual oasis, a place where the beauty of the monastic life could flourish, even in the harshest of environments.

Work began immediately. Monks and volunteers labored tirelessly, digging wells, planting gardens, and building the first structures. The elder's vision was to create a self-sustaining community where prayer, work, and hospitality were interwoven into daily life. Under the guidance of Elder Ephraim, the barren desert began to blossom. Trees were planted, fountains built, and chapels erected. Soon, the once-dry ground was transformed into a verdant sanctuary, filled with olive groves, citrus orchards, and blooming flowers. The air became filled with the sweet scent of jasmine and the sound of birds singing among the trees.

St. Anthony's Monastery became a spiritual haven for thousands of pilgrims seeking solace, healing, and spiritual renewal. People from all walks of life came to see the desert miracle, to walk among the beautiful gardens, to attend the long, contemplative services, and to seek the elder's wisdom. Many spoke of miracles—of physical healing, of emotional restoration, of broken lives made whole again.

But St. Anthony's was only the beginning. Elder Ephraim went on to found other monasteries, each one a jewel in the crown of American Orthodoxy. One such foundation is the Monastery of the Theotokos, the Life-Giving Spring in Dunlap, California.

A Spiritual Oasis in California

Nestled in the rolling foothills of the Sierra Nevada, the Monastery of the Life-Giving Spring sits like a gem, hidden among tall pines and ancient oaks. The sunlight filters through the leaves, casting dappled shadows on the stone paths that wind their way through the gardens. The sound of water trickles softly from a spring, the very spring that inspired the monastery's name.

I visited Life-Giving Spring Monastery on a warm summer day in 2017, eager to experience this place I had heard so much about. As I approached, I felt a sense of peace wash over me,

Monastery of the Theotokos, the Life-Giving Spring, in Dunlap, California

a calm that seemed to emanate from the very ground. I was greeted by Mother Markella, the abbess, whose warm smile and gentle demeanor immediately put me at ease.

Mother Markella took me on a tour of the grounds, sharing stories of the monastery's founding and the miracles that had accompanied its development. "This place is a gift," she said, her eyes bright with enthusiasm. "Elder Ephraim saw that this land could become a spiritual oasis, a place where people could come to find God, to reconnect with the beauty of His creation, and to renew their spirits."

The monastery, like St. Anthony's in Arizona, had begun with a simple vision and a lot of hard work. But through prayer, perseverance, and the elder's guidance, it had grown into a thriving community of nuns who lived a life of prayer, hospitality, and service. The monastery's chapel, a simple yet beautiful structure adorned with icons and filled with the warm glow of candlelight, was a place of profound stillness, a place where one could feel the presence of God in every corner.

Mother Markella spoke to me about the power of monastic life, about the beauty of simplicity, of waking each day with the sole purpose of seeking God. "We are not here to escape the world," she explained, "but to live in it differently, to live a life that is wholly dedicated to God."

I felt a deep connection to the words she spoke, a realization that this was not just a different way of living but a deeper way of seeing, of understanding the world and one's place in it.

The Monastic Revival in North America

The monasteries founded by Elder Ephraim, from St. Anthony's in Arizona to Life-Giving Spring in California and many others, represent a profound monastic revival in North America. These monasteries have become spiritual centers where the ancient traditions of Orthodox monasticism are not only preserved but are being lived out in a way that speaks to the needs of our time.

Elder Ephraim's monasteries are places where people can come to experience the beauty of Orthodoxy, where the rhythms of monastic life provide a counterpoint to the rush and noise of modern existence. The monks and nuns who live in these communities embody a different way of being—a life of prayer, humility, and self-denial that challenges the values of the world around us.

The power of monastic life, as Elder Ephraim taught, is rooted in a deep connection to the early Desert Fathers such as St. Anthony of Egypt, who is often called the father of monasticism. St. Anthony left his home in the city and retreated to the desert, seeking solitude and communion with God. His life of asceticism, prayer, and spiritual warfare became a model for countless others who sought to live a life wholly devoted to Christ.

Elder Ephraim often spoke of St. Anthony's example, seeing in it a guide for the revival of monasticism in America. Just as St. Anthony had gone into the desert to find God, so too had Elder Ephraim come to the deserts of Arizona and the hills of California, believing that these places, far from the distractions of the city, could become new centers of spiritual renewal.

The miracles associated with Elder Ephraim and his monasteries are numerous. People have reported healings, both physical and spiritual, after visiting these holy sites. There are stories of hearts being softened, relationships being healed, and lives being transformed. It is said that Elder Ephraim, even in his old age, possessed the gift of discernment, the ability to see into the souls of those who came to him, to understand their struggles, and to offer them guidance with love and compassion.

The Beauty and Power of Monastic Life

The sun was beginning to set as I made my way back from Life-Giving Spring Monastery, the sky ablaze with color, the air cool and crisp. I thought about the monks and nuns I had met, about the beauty of their life, the peace that seemed to radiate from them. I thought about Elder Ephraim, a man who had left everything behind to follow Christ, who had come to this country with nothing but a prayer and a vision, and who had built something extraordinary.

The monasteries founded by Elder Ephraim are not just places of refuge; they are places of transformation. They are places where people come to find healing, to reconnect with their faith, to rediscover the beauty of a life lived for God. They are places where the spirit of the Desert Fathers lives on, where the ancient traditions of Orthodoxy are kept alive in a world that is constantly changing.

As I drove away, I felt a sense of gratitude, a sense that I had been given a glimpse into something sacred, something that could not be fully captured in words. The beauty of these monasteries, the miracles of their founding, the wisdom of Elder

Ephraim—all of it pointed to a deeper truth, a truth that transcends time and space, a truth that speaks to the very heart of what it means to be human.

Monastic life, as Elder Ephraim taught, is not just for the monks and nuns who live it; it is for all of us. It is a reminder that there is another way to live, a way that is deeper, richer, and more meaningful than anything the world has to offer. It is a call to seek God with all our hearts, to let go of the things that hold us back, and to embrace the life that He has called us to live.

Elder Ephraim's legacy lives on in the monasteries he founded, in the lives he touched, and in the hearts of all who seek to follow Christ more deeply. His life was a testament to the power of prayer, the beauty of humility, and the joy of living for God. Through his example, we are reminded that the monastic life is not just a relic of the past, but a living, breathing reality that continues to inspire and transform lives today.

Holy Elder Ephraim, pray to God for us!

The Native American Journey to Orthodoxy

FINDING FAITH IN THE ANCIENT CHURCH

Sacred Alaska:
A Living Testament to Faith and Culture

The windswept tundras of Alaska, the towering spruce forests, and the icy waters of the Bering Sea hold stories older than memory itself—stories of resilience, survival, and spirituality deeply woven into the fabric of the Native Alaskan experience. These are not merely tales of the past but living narratives that continue to shape the lives of the people who call this land home. When I first watched the documentary *Sacred Alaska*, I felt as though I had been transported into a mystical realm where the sacred and the natural were inextricably intertwined. The film did not merely narrate history; it breathed life into it. This breathtaking exploration of Native Alaskan spirituality and the profound influence of Orthodox Christianity became the seed of inspiration for my book and film project, *American Orthodox*.

Sacred Alaska, directed by Simon Scionka and produced by Silas Karbo, is an award-winning visual symphony that captures the unique fusion of Native Alaskan indigenous spirituality and Orthodox Christianity. Its powerful storytelling and stunning cinematography make the harsh, beautiful Alaskan wilderness a character in its own right. As I sat mesmerized by the images on the screen—snowy peaks standing like sentinels under an infinite sky, rivers winding through untamed wilderness, and humble wooden churches glowing with candlelight—I understood that this was more than a film. It was an icon, a sacred window into a world where faith and culture converge to sanctify the land and its people.

The Saints of Alaska: Voices from the Sacred Past

The documentary opens with the arrival of St. Herman and nine other Russian Orthodox monks on Kodiak Island on September 24, 1794. Their journey from the remote monasteries of Valaam, Russia, across Siberia, and over the perilous icy waters of the Bering Sea is told with reverence and drama. As the film recounts, these monks did not come merely as colonizers or proselytizers; they came as sanctifiers, bringing with them the gospel of Christ to a land that already carried a profound sense of the sacred.

St. Herman, known as Grandpa to the Native Alaskans for his warmth and approachability, emerges as the heart of the story. The film portrays him not only as a holy man but as a fierce advocate for justice. He fought against the exploitation of Native Alaskans by the Russian-American Company and its governor, Alexander Baranov. St. Herman's love for the people he served is palpable in the documentary, particularly in the stories of his joyful interactions with children and his tireless efforts to protect the vulnerable. The image of him baking cookies for the children of Kodiak, juxtaposed with his profound asceticism on Spruce Island, captures the paradox of his sanctity: at once deeply human and entirely otherworldly.

Another luminous figure in *Sacred Alaska* is St. Innocent of Alaska, the Enlightener of the Aleuts and Apostle to America. The film vividly depicts his missionary journeys, traveling by kayak across the treacherous waters to reach the most remote corners of Alaska. St. Innocent's dedication to translating Orthodox texts into Native languages and his tireless work to bridge cultural divides illustrate the incarnational nature of his mission. His story, as told in the film, is a testament to the transformative power of humility and perseverance.

St. Yakov Netsvetov, the first Native Alaskan ordained to the priesthood, is also prominently featured. His efforts to minister to his own people, often under extreme conditions, are portrayed with both historical accuracy and emotional depth. The film captures his role as a bridge between the Orthodox faith and Native Alaskan culture, a role that continues to resonate in the hearts of his spiritual descendants.

Matushka Olga: The Hidden Saint of the Tundra

Among the saints highlighted in *Sacred Alaska* is Matushka Olga Michael of Kwethluk, whose life exemplifies the sanctity found in simplicity and service. Born into the Yup'ik culture,

Matushka Olga was a wife, mother of nine, midwife, and spiritual guide. The film interviews her family members and community, who speak of her gentle wisdom, tireless care for women and children, and deep prayer life. Even before her official canonization, those who knew her recognized her as a saint.

Her story struck a particular chord with me. The idea that holiness could be found not only in monastic seclusion but in the ordinary rhythms of family life, in hidden acts of kindness and compassion, resonated deeply. Matushka Olga's life, as portrayed in the documentary, is a living icon of what it means to bring the sacred into the everyday. Her legacy invites us to look for God not in the extraordinary but in the seemingly mundane, to sanctify the world around us through love and service.

The Sacred Bond Between Faith and Land

One of the most compelling aspects of *Sacred Alaska* is its exploration of the intrinsic connection between Native Alaskan spirituality and Orthodox Christianity. Native Alaskans have always viewed the land, animals, and waters as sacred, interconnected elements of creation. The film portrays how the Orthodox faith, with its sacramental worldview, was not imposed upon them as something foreign but embraced as the fulfillment of their deepest spiritual intuitions.

Through interviews with Native Alaskans, Orthodox clergy, and monastics, the documentary reveals how this fusion of faith and culture has created a uniquely Alaskan Orthodoxy. Prayers are sung in Native languages, traditions are preserved within the liturgical life of the Church, and the saints of Alaska are venerated not just as historical figures but as living intercessors who continue to guide their people. This harmonious blending of the ancient Christian faith with indigenous traditions offers a model of evangelism rooted in respect, patience, and genuine love.

The Cinematic Power of Sacred Alaska

The visual storytelling of *Sacred Alaska* is nothing short of breathtaking. Director Simon Scionka and producer Silas Karbo masterfully weave together historical narrative, personal testimonies, and awe-inspiring footage of Alaska's natural beauty. The snow-covered peaks, dense forests, and serene waters become more than a backdrop; they are integral to the story, reflecting the grandeur and mystery of the Creator.

The filmmakers' commitment to authenticity shines through in every frame. Interviews with Native Alaskans are interspersed with scenes of traditional dances, subsistence fishing, and community gatherings, offering a glimpse into a way of life that is both ancient and enduring. The juxtaposition of these scenes with the solemnity of Orthodox liturgical services creates a powerful mosaic that speaks to the universality of faith and the sanctity of creation.

Inspiration for American Orthodox

Watching *Sacred Alaska* was a turning point for me. The film's exploration of the sanctification of land, the legacy of saints, and the fusion of faith and culture awakened something deep within me. It was as though the stories of St. Herman, St. Innocent, and Matushka Olga had reached across the centuries to call me to action. Their lives, so deeply rooted in humility and love, inspired me to explore the ways in which Orthodoxy has taken root in other corners of America.

This inspiration became the foundation for *American Orthodox*, both the book and the documentary. Like *Sacred Alaska*, my project seeks to illuminate the stories of saints, holy places, and faithful communities, showing how the ancient faith continues to transform lives in the modern world. The themes of sanctification, cultural harmony, and the universality of Orthodoxy that resonated so strongly in *Sacred Alaska* have become the guiding principles of my own work.

A Call to See the Sacred

As the final scenes of *Sacred Alaska* fade into the serene landscapes of the Alaskan wilderness, the viewer is left with a sense of wonder and a profound question: How can we, too, live lives that sanctify the world around us? The film is not just a celebration of Native Alaskan Orthodoxy but an invitation to see the sacred in our own lives, to honor the land, care for one another, and live in communion with God.

The story of Orthodoxy in Alaska is a testament to the enduring power of faith to transform not only individuals but entire cultures. It is a story that reminds us that holiness is not confined to any one place or people but is found wherever hearts are open to the grace of God. Watching *Sacred Alaska* was not just an experience; it was a pilgrimage—a journey into the heart of a sacred land that continues to call us to a deeper understanding of faith, culture, and the beauty of creation.

Stories of Indigenous Converts to Orthodoxy

The stillness of the forest was broken only by the gentle rustle of leaves and the soft patter of footsteps on the damp earth. A solitary figure walked with a steady, rhythmic gait, his long hair tied back, a cross around his neck catching the light filtering through the canopy above. He was Vladimir Natawe, an Orthodox Christian and the spiritual leader of his Mohawk tribe, who had discovered a deep connection between his Native traditions and the ancient faith of the Orthodox Church. It was a journey marked by mystery, revelation, and a quiet courage that defied centuries of oppression and misunderstanding.

Vladimir's journey to Orthodoxy began in the twilight of his life, a journey that had taken him far from the reservations of his youth, deep into the heart of an ancient faith that touched his soul in ways he had never imagined. He often spoke of his path to Orthodoxy as a "secret path," a hidden trail that wound through the dense forests of his heritage and led him to the Church.

One evening in the Russian Cathedral of Saints Peter and Paul, as Vespers was just beginning, a young Greek named Yannis spotted Vladimir, his presence distinct and striking amid the congregation. Yannis was drawn to him, sensing a story hidden behind those deep-set eyes and strong features. After the service, he approached Vladimir, eager to know more about this Native American who seemed so at home in an Orthodox church.

"Yannis," Vladimir greeted him warmly. "Welcome."

Yannis asked, "And you? What brings you here?"

To his surprise, Vladimir replied with a phrase in Greek that translates to "In the beginning was the Logos and the Logos was with God, and God was the Logos" (John 1:1).

Vladimir went on to explain his unique spiritual journey. Born into a Mohawk tribe near Montreal, his people had been coerced into Roman Catholicism by European missionaries in the eighteenth century. These conversions were often made with a "noose around the neck," as he described it, trampling on centuries-old traditions. By the age of thirty-two, he could no longer tolerate this forced duality of being "Roman Catholic by day and Indian by night," so he sought his own path. His intellectual curiosity led him to study linguistics and, in turn, the lives of Saints Cyril and Methodius, the Apostles to the Slavs. His fascination with language opened his eyes to Orthodoxy.

Vladimir attended Vespers at an Orthodox church out of curiosity and was captivated by the richness of the liturgy, the beauty of the icons, and the familiarity he sensed in the prayers and rituals. "It felt like I had discovered the 'secret path,'" he would often say. Born to full-blooded Mohawk parents in Kahnawake, near Montreal, Quebec, Canada, his birthname was Frank Natawe. He found deep parallels between Native traditions and Orthodox spirituality, and eventually he was baptized into the faith, taking the name Vladimir.

For years, Vladimir lived a double life, leading his people by day and attending Orthodox services by night. He remained their spiritual leader, officiating at weddings and funerals, listening to their problems in the "long house," and guiding them with wisdom he drew from both his Native heritage and his Orthodox faith. His life was a quiet testimony to the bridge that could be built between two seemingly disparate worlds, a bridge made of humility, love, and a deep yearning for truth.

The Role of Saints and Local Leaders in the Native American Orthodox Journey

Orthodoxy's encounter with Native Americans is not a recent phenomenon; it began long before Vladimir's time, with the earliest Russian Orthodox missionaries to Alaska in the late eighteenth century. The Alaskan Natives, like the Kodiak Aleuts, were among the first indigenous peoples of North America to embrace Orthodoxy. They received the faith not through coercion but through the humble examples of men like St. Herman of Alaska, St. Innocent, and St. Juvenaly, who lived among them, learned their languages, and served them with great love.

St. Herman, a monk from Valaam Monastery in Russia, arrived on Kodiak Island in 1794 and became a defender and protector of the Native people against the abuses of the Russian-American Company. He advocated for their rights, cared for the sick, and taught them the Christian faith in a way that resonated with their spiritual traditions. His presence was a living example of Christ's love, and many Aleuts converted to Orthodoxy, seeing in him a true friend and protector.

St. Innocent, another great missionary, traveled across the vast expanses of Alaska, establishing churches and schools, translating the Scriptures and liturgical texts into the Native languages, and training indigenous clergy. His commitment to the Native peoples was unwavering, and he was beloved for his humility, wisdom, and tireless dedication.

The Orthodox Church in Alaska grew steadily, becoming a spiritual home for many Natives. It was during a time of great hardship and suffering, particularly during the era when Natives were forcibly enrolled in boarding schools, that Orthodox priests, many of whom were Native or of mixed Native and Russian descent, became defenders of their communities. They advocated for the children, challenged unjust policies, and helped preserve Native languages and traditions within an Orthodox context.

Today, the Orthodox Church in Alaska continues to be a spiritual refuge for many indigenous peoples. The Faith has been woven into the fabric of their lives, offering comfort, guidance, and a sense of continuity with their ancestors. The beauty of Orthodox worship—with its chants, icons, incense, and ancient prayers—speaks deeply to the Native spirit, which has always been attuned to the sacredness of creation and the presence of the Divine.

The Witness of Rebecca Hernandez: Embracing Orthodoxy as a Native American

Rebecca Hernandez, also known as Petka after her patron saint, St. Paraskeva, is another remarkable example of the Native American journey to Orthodoxy. Born into a large, devout Christian family in Los Angeles, Rebecca grew up in the Baptist tradition, deeply immersed in the Bible and church life. Her mother was Mescalero Apache and her father was Mexican-American, giving her a rich cultural heritage.

Rebecca's path to Orthodoxy was winding and complex. She attended a Catholic college and fell in love with Catholicism's rituals and traditions, converting despite her family's hesitation. However, a chance discovery would change her life forever. While working as an intern at the Southwest Museum in Los Angeles, she stumbled upon a box of old slides depicting Aleut Orthodox services and clergy in Alaska. Intrigued, she decided to investigate further.

She found her way to St. Steven's Serbian Orthodox Cathedral in Alhambra, California, and began attending services, drawn by the depth and beauty of Orthodox worship. Over five years, she gradually embraced Orthodoxy, despite many difficult conversations with her Catholic mentors and friends. She found in Orthodoxy a depth of tradition and a sense of timelessness that resonated with her spirit.

Rebecca is now an advocate for Orthodoxy among Native Americans and for Native Americans within the Orthodox community. She has traveled to Alaska to attend the Feast of St. Herman, where she experienced the liturgy led by Aleut clergy in their own language—a profound moment that connected her with the rich history of Native Orthodox Christians. She continues to work as a community archivist, preserving Native history and culture while fostering connections between Native Americans and the Orthodox Church.

Connecting Native Traditions with the Ancient Faith

Many Native American converts to Orthodoxy, like Vladimir and Rebecca, find a deep resonance between their indigenous traditions and the teachings of the Orthodox Church. They see in Orthodoxy a faith that respects mystery, honors creation, and understands the spiritual journey as a path of humility, repentance, and communion with God.

For example, one of many Native tribal concepts of "the Great Mystery" aligns closely with the Orthodox understanding of God as both transcendent and immanent, a divine presence that fills all things yet is beyond all things. The Native tradition of offering sweet-smelling herbs and smoke in prayer parallels the Orthodox practice of offering incense to God. Both traditions emphasize the importance of facing east in prayer, honoring the direction of the rising sun, which symbolizes the Resurrection of Christ.

One of the most profound parallels can be seen in the Native understanding of walking in a "sacred manner." An old Native holy man once said, "Every step you take on earth should be a prayer." This idea mirrors the Orthodox call to pray without ceasing, to make every moment of life an offering to God. It reflects a shared understanding that all of creation is sacred, that every action can become a prayer when done with a heart open to the Divine.

A New Chapter: Native American Orthodoxy Today

Today, Native American Orthodoxy is experiencing a quiet but steady revival. Communities like Orthodox Native America are dedicated to sharing the Orthodox faith with Native Americans, building bridges between cultures, and fostering a deeper understanding of the ancient Church's teachings.

This movement is not about replacing or erasing Native traditions but about fulfilling them in the light of Christ. As Vladimir Natawe once observed, "I see parallels between our traditions and the Orthodox tradition. This discovery fulfilled my Indian ethos and supplemented it."

By embracing Orthodoxy, many Native Americans find a way to reconnect with their own heritage while deepening their relationship with God. They discover in the Church a spiritual home where their unique cultural expressions are not only welcomed but celebrated. They see in the lives of Native saints like St. Yakov Netsvetov, St. Peter the Aleut, and St. Olga of Alaska a continuity of faith and tradition that speaks to their deepest longings.

The Native American journey to Orthodoxy is a testament to the universality of the Gospel, to the truth that Christ came for all people, in all times, in all places. It is a reminder that the ancient faith of the Orthodox Church has the power to speak to every heart, to touch every soul, and to bring light to every corner of the earth.

May the prayers of St. Peter the Aleut, St. Olga, and all the Native saints continue to guide us on our journey, bringing us closer to the heart of God, closer to each other, and closer to the mystery of His love.

The author with Fr. Moses Berry

The African American Experience

A PATH TO ORTHODOXY

Personal Stories of Conversion and Spiritual Growth

The scent of incense permeated the air, mingling with the warm glow of candles, their soft light flickering across the ancient icons. I stood in the back of the church, my heart pounding as the choir's voices rose in harmonious unity, chanting prayers in a language that was not my own but somehow felt deeply familiar. This was the Orthodox Church, and though its traditions were new to me, they resonated with an ancient truth, an echo of something I had been searching for all my life.

My journey to Orthodoxy began in California as I moved through various churches, each offering a unique glimpse into the beauty and depth of the Orthodox faith. My first visit was to the Ascension Greek Orthodox Cathedral in Oakland, where I was captivated by the richness of the liturgical traditions and the depth of the hymns. I then found myself at Holy Ascension Russian Orthodox Church in Sacramento, a small community that welcomed me with warmth and kindness and whose devotion to the faith drew me closer.

At Assumption of the Blessed Virgin Mary Serbian Orthodox Church in Sacramento, I encountered another expression of Orthodoxy—old-world tradition meeting new-world openness. I was particularly moved by the warmth and generosity of the parishioners who shared their faith and lives with me. My journey also led me to St. Sava Serbian Orthodox Church in Jackson, where I was struck by the resilience and strength of a community that had weathered many storms yet stood firm in its faith.

Finally, I found my spiritual home at Elevation of the Holy Cross, an Orthodox Church in America (OCA) parish in Sacramento, where the services are conducted in English, and most of the parishioners and clergy are converts like myself. Here, I found a community of seekers, people who, like me, had come from many different backgrounds, drawn to the ancient faith of the Orthodox Church.

Father Raphael Morgan, the First African American Orthodox Priest

Hidden within the folds of time lies the remarkable story of Father Raphael Morgan, a man whose life journey carried him across oceans, continents, and faiths. Born Robert Josias Morgan in the vibrant landscapes of Chapelton, Clarendon Parish, Jamaica, sometime between 1864 and 1871, his story began with loss—his father's death six months before his birth.

The African American Experience

Raised in the Anglican tradition by his mother, Mary Ann Morgan, young Robert exhibited an early thirst for knowledge and spiritual exploration. This longing propelled him to distant shores, from Colón, Panama, to British Honduras, before returning to Jamaica. Later, his footsteps led him to the United States and then England, as he pursued his quest for spiritual truth, a quest that would ultimately reshape the fabric of American Orthodoxy.

Robert's path to Orthodoxy was neither simple nor direct. After serving as a minister in the African Methodist Episcopal Church and studying in Sierra Leone, he found himself drawn deeper into the mysteries of faith. Immersing himself in Greek, Latin, and theological studies, he questioned his Anglican and AME roots, seeking a fuller truth. In 1907, his journey culminated in Constantinople, where he was baptized Raphael and ordained as the first African American Orthodox Christian priest. His ordination by the Holy Synod marked a historic moment, one that carried both hope and weighty expectations as he was sent back to America to establish the Orthodox faith among English speakers.

In Philadelphia, Fr. Raphael founded the Orthodox Community of All Saints, a pioneering attempt to create a space where Orthodox doctrine could be taught in English, making the faith accessible to a wider audience. With the support of former Episcopalian and Methodist clergy, he aimed to build schools and churches to anchor this growing community. Yet, his mission was fraught with challenges. The community's ultimate fate remains unclear, a poignant reminder of the uphill battle faced by early Orthodox pioneers in America.

Fr. Raphael's life was not without personal struggles. His marriage to Charlotte Morgan ended in a contentious divorce, marred by accusations of cruelty and infidelity. The mystery of his daughter, taken to Greece as a child, further deepened the complexities of his story. Despite these trials, his legacy endures as a testament to resilience. Fr. Raphael's pioneering spirit broke racial and cultural barriers, offering a vision of Orthodoxy that embraced the unique spiritual heritage of African Americans while staying rooted in the ancient traditions of the faith.

Today, his influence resonates in the lives of figures like Fr. Moses Berry and the Fellowship of St. Moses the Black. Fr. Moses, through his own ministry, carries forward the work Fr. Raphael began, bridging the deep spiritual traditions of Orthodoxy with the transformative narratives of African American history. Together, their stories illuminate the enduring power of faith to unite and transform, reminding us that the journey to spiritual truth, though often fraught with difficulty, is a journey worth taking.

The Life and Witness of Father Moses Berry

In many ways, my own search mirrors the transformative journey of Father Moses Berry, a man whose life is a testament to the unexpected turns that lead to grace. Born Karl Berry in Ash Grove, Missouri, Father Moses did not grow up in an Orthodox family. His story begins in a small town steeped in the dark history of American slavery. Father Moses' ancestry includes Nathaniel Boone, the son of the legendary American frontiersman Daniel Boone, and Maria Boone, an enslaved woman. The Ozark Foothills African-American History Museum, which

Father Moses founded in his hometown, houses faded portraits, artifacts, and heirlooms that tell the story of his ancestors' struggle for survival.

Like me, Father Moses felt the pull of something more profound than his immediate surroundings offered. At age fifteen, he left Ash Grove and hitchhiked to California, chasing the promise of the "flower power" movement. In California, he lived in communes, learned to roll hashish, and played in a band called Honey Chile. However, the life he sought in the countercultural scene led him to unexpected places, and after opening an underground coffee shop that doubled as a front for selling hashish and marijuana, he found himself in prison, in solitary confinement, praying desperately for a second chance.

Father Moses' prayers were answered. After his release, his journey took him to New York City, where he became a teacher in Harlem and met his wife, a liberal Jewish woman. They were searching together, just as I was when I first walked into that Orthodox church, unsure of what I would find but open to the possibilities. They were invited to a small Orthodox chapel in Richmond, Virginia, where Moses was captivated by the beauty of the liturgy, the poetry of the prayers, and the reverence of the worship. He described it as a moment of deep recognition—a realization that he had found a spiritual home.

Returning to Ash Grove, Father Moses dedicated his life to serving God. He founded the Ozark Foothills African-American History Museum and began ministering to at-risk youth, prisoners, and drug addicts. He also founded Mother of Unexpected Joy, a small Orthodox church in a white and red barn with a golden onion dome, nestled in the middle of a cornfield. The church stands as a beacon of hope in a world often filled with despair.

Father Moses' legacy is not just in the stories he told but in the lives he touched. He was a living example of God's grace, and his work reminds us that even the most unlikely people can become vessels of God's love. As I reflected on his life, I realized how much our journeys had in common—both of us finding Orthodoxy in unexpected places, both of us transformed by its beauty and truth.

Modern Voices: Father Turbo Qualls, Father Samuel Davis, and Others

The African American Orthodox community is growing, and its voices are diverse and rich in their experiences. Father Turbo Qualls, a former punk rocker and tattoo artist turned Orthodox priest, has become a dynamic voice for Orthodoxy among African Americans, especially through his online presence. His YouTube channel, The Royal Path, reaches a new generation with a message of authenticity, hope, and spiritual depth. His journey from the counterculture to the Orthodox Church speaks to many who feel disconnected from traditional religious expressions.

Father Turbo's story is one of profound transformation. Born into a challenging environment, he found himself navigating the complexities of life in the inner city. His early years were marked by rebellion and a search for meaning in the countercultural world of punk rock and tattoo artistry. These experiences, though unconventional, instilled in him a sensitivity to the struggles and pain of those on the margins of society. They also served as a crucible for his eventual spiritual awakening.

Before embracing Orthodoxy, Father Turbo worked as an alcohol and drug counselor, offering guidance to those battling addiction. This work not only deepened his compassion for those in despair but also laid the foundation for his pastoral ministry. His ability to connect with people from all walks of life, especially those who feel forgotten or rejected, has become one of the hallmarks of his priesthood.

Now serving as the pastor of St. Mary of Egypt Orthodox Church in Kansas City, Missouri, Father Turbo brings his unique blend of authenticity, empathy, and spiritual wisdom to his parishioners. Located in the heart of the inner city, St. Mary's is more than a church—it is a sanctuary for those seeking healing and hope. Under Father Turbo's leadership, the parish has become a vibrant community that reflects the transformative power of the Orthodox faith.

Father Turbo's ministry extends beyond the walls of his parish. His online presence through The Royal Path allows him to reach a global audience, sharing the timeless wisdom of Orthodoxy in a way that resonates with contemporary seekers. His message is clear: the ancient faith of the Church is not only relevant but essential in addressing the spiritual crises of modern life. Through his engaging and heartfelt talks, Father Turbo invites his listeners to embark on their own journey of transformation, drawing them closer to the light of Christ.

At the heart of Father Turbo's work is a commitment to making Orthodoxy accessible to those who may feel excluded or alienated by traditional religious structures. His life is a testament to the idea that no one is beyond the reach of God's love and that the Church is a home for all who seek truth, healing, and redemption. Through his ministry, Father Turbo Qualls stands as a living example of the Church's mission to bring the Gospel to all people, particularly those in need of hope and renewal.

Father Samuel Davis, the first African American priest ordained in the OCA, shares a powerful story of conversion that speaks to the complexities of racial identity and faith. A former Baptist minister, Father Samuel embraced Orthodoxy as a fulfillment of his lifelong search for the ancient faith. He often recounts the moment he first walked into an Orthodox church and felt the overwhelming presence of the Holy Spirit, a moment that changed his life forever.

Father Paul Abernathy, another prominent African American Orthodox leader, founded the Neighborhood Resilience Project in Pittsburgh, focusing on community building and outreach to the marginalized. He is the author of the book, *Prayer of the Broken Heart: An Orthodox Christian Reflection on African American Spirituality* (Ancient Faith Publishing, 2021) and is featured in the PBS documentary *Made in America*. His work highlights the social dimensions of the faith, a call to live out the Gospel in every aspect of life. Father Paul's efforts are a testament to how Orthodoxy can serve as a bridge between faith and social justice, bringing healing and hope to those in need.

Father Nathaniel Johnson, a man of deep faith and extraordinary talent, once moved audiences with his skill as a professional jazz musician. But the rhythms of his life took a profound turn when he heard the call to serve Christ in the Orthodox

Church. For years, Fr. Nathaniel faithfully served St. Lawrence Orthodox Church in the redwood-shrouded hills of Felton, California, where his gentle and vibrant personality brought the gospel to life for a diverse congregation. Now retired, he resides in Goldendale, Washington, where he continues to share his wisdom, joy, and love of music with all who seek his counsel. His journey from the world of jazz to the priesthood is a testament to the transformative power of God's call and the beauty of a life dedicated to service.

Father Martin Johnson, another notable figure among African American Orthodox clergy, found his vocation through years of military service as a US Navy chaplain, offering spiritual guidance to sailors and Marines in some of the most challenging of life's circumstances. Now serving as the rector for St. Anthony Antiochian Orthodox Church in Butler, Pennsylvania, Fr. Martin brings the same strength of pastoral experience and compassion to his ministry, guiding pilgrims from all walks of life who visit their parish to new insights in faith while building and fostering a community of learning and renewal. He serves on the board at St. Tikhon Orthodox Theological Seminary and works with young adults at the various Orthodox camps in the US. Married to Melinda Johnson, the CEO of Ancient Faith Ministries, he exemplifies the dynamic interplay of faith and leadership, serving as a bridge between Orthodoxy's ancient traditions and its growing presence in modern America.

Fr. Nathaniel and Fr. Martin represent the profound contributions of African American Orthodox clergy to the life of the Church. From the jazz clubs of California to the chaplaincy of the US Navy, their journeys reflect the breadth of experiences and gifts that have enriched Orthodox Christianity in America. Like Fr. Moses Berry, Fr. Turbo Qualls, Fr. Paul Abernathy, and Fr. Samuel Davis, they embody a living witness to the unity of the Church in Christ, drawing all people toward the fullness of the faith with their unique gifts and tireless devotion. Their stories illuminate the vibrant tapestry of Orthodoxy in America, offering hope and inspiration to all who encounter them.

Connecting to Ancient African Saints: Saint Moses the Black and Others

The desert sun blazed high overhead, scorching the sand beneath Moses' feet as he sprinted through the arid landscape, his breath ragged, his heart pounding like a drumbeat in his chest. Behind him, the shouts of his pursuers grew louder, the sharp clang of swords and the heavy thud of footsteps echoing across the barren land. Dust kicked up around him as he ran, his dark eyes scanning the horizon for a place to hide. He knew this life well—this life of pursuit and escape, of shadows and violence. He was Moses the Black, the most feared bandit in the Nile Valley, a man of ruthless reputation. And now, his own crimes had driven him to the brink.

The failed robbery weighed heavily on his mind; he had underestimated his prey this time. Desperation clawed at him as he reached the edge of a rocky outcrop and saw, in the distance, a small cluster of mud-brick buildings—the desert monastery of Scetis. With no other place to go, he stumbled toward it, panting, his powerful frame now trembling with exhaustion. He burst through the gates and into the quiet courtyard, collapsing at the feet of an old monk, the abbot, St. Isidore. The monks stood back, wary and watchful, but Isidore looked down at the breathless, broken man before him.

"Brother," Isidore spoke softly, his voice like a calm breeze against the roar of Moses' inner turmoil, "why have you come here?"

Moses' eyes met the abbot's, and for the first time in his life, he felt a flicker of something he could not name—something like hope. In that moment, amid the stark silence of the desert, the seeds of his transformation were planted.

From that desperate beginning, Saint Moses the Black would go on to live a life that resonates deeply with many African American Orthodox Christians today. A former slave and robber turned monk and priest in fourth-century Egypt, St. Moses' life is a powerful example of repentance, forgiveness, and transformation. Known for his humility, wisdom, and deep faith, St. Moses became a beloved figure in the monastic community of Scetis, Egypt. His life challenges us to see beyond our past mistakes and embrace the mercy of God, who welcomes all who turn to Him with a contrite heart.

Born in Ethiopia, Moses was a tall, powerful man whose strength and cunning made him a leader among bandits. As a former slave, he harbored deep anger and bitterness, turning to a life of violence and robbery. He led a ruthless gang that terrorized the Nile Valley, plundering villages and instilling fear in the hearts of many. His reputation grew as a man who seemed beyond redemption—a wild, untamable force with a thirst for power.

But something stirred within Moses' hardened heart, a flicker of a desire for something more profound than the life he was leading, when he sought refuge among the monks of the desert monastery in Scetis, Egypt. There he encountered the abbot, St. Isidore, who saw through the outer shell of brutality and discerned a soul longing for peace. Under Isidore's gentle guidance, Moses began to confront his own inner demons. Over time, his fierce exterior began to soften as he committed himself to a life of repentance and prayer.

Moses underwent a radical transformation. He abandoned his old ways, exchanging his sword for the humble robes of a monk. His journey of repentance was not easy; the temptations of his past often haunted him. Yet he persisted, throwing himself into the rigorous ascetic practices of the monastic life, fasting, and offering prayers for the forgiveness of his sins. Through his struggles, Moses became known for his deep humility and profound wisdom, his rough edges slowly smoothed by the grace of God.

His life became a testimony to the power of God's mercy. When another monk asked him how to achieve purity of heart, Moses famously poured a jug of dirty water into a bowl and said, "The soul is like this water. If left undisturbed, it will become clear, but if stirred, it will remain cloudy." He was beloved by his fellow monks, who saw in him a true example of the possibility of redemption.

In his later years, Moses was ordained as a priest, serving with love and dedication in the same monastic community where he had once sought refuge. However, his end came as dramatically as his life's transformation. At the age of seventy-five, he was warned that a group of Berber bandits was coming to raid the monastery. Moses refused to flee, saying, "It is I who brought violence upon this place, and now it is my time to lay down my life." He stood his ground, calmly awaiting death, and was martyred along with seven other monks.

Saint Moses the Black's story is one of dramatic transformation, a journey from darkness to light that reminds us of the boundless mercy and love of God. His life challenges us to look beyond our past mistakes, knowing that God welcomes all who come to Him with a contrite heart.

Saint Moses' example connects with other African saints whose stories continue to inspire modern seekers. Saint Cyprian of Carthage, a third-century bishop and theologian, wrote extensively on the unity of the Church and the importance of pastoral care. His writings offer profound insights for those looking to deepen their spiritual life and understanding of the Church's role in the world.

Saint Simon of Cyrene, who carried the cross of Christ, is remembered as a symbol of compassion and shared suffering. For many African Americans, his story is a reminder of the dignity and honor to be found in bearing burdens for others, a theme that resonates deeply with the historical experiences of the African diaspora.

Saint Mary of Egypt: A Journey of Redemption

The city of Alexandria in the 5th century was a bustling hub of culture, commerce, and indulgence, where the ancient and the decadent collided. Amidst its sun-drenched streets and vibrant markets lived a young woman named Mary. From an early age,

Mary embodied the hedonistic spirit of the city. Her beauty was striking, and she used it as a weapon, luring men into her web not for financial gain but for the sheer thrill of conquest. She lived without boundaries, reveling in her own freedom, unshackled by societal expectations or moral constraints.

For seventeen years, Mary embraced this life of reckless abandon, taking pleasure wherever she could find it. Yet, beneath the surface of her unrestrained existence lay an emptiness she could neither name nor escape. The laughter and ecstasy she shared with her companions faded quickly into the silence of her solitary nights. The allure of sin, which once burned so brightly, began to dull, leaving her searching for something deeper, something lasting.

One fateful day, the city buzzed with the excitement of a pilgrimage to Jerusalem. A ship full of pilgrims was bound for the Holy Land to celebrate the Exaltation of the Holy Cross. Mary, intrigued by the throngs of travelers and eager for a new adventure, decided to join them. She boarded the vessel, not as a fellow pilgrim, but with the intention of seducing as many travelers as she could during the journey. Her motives were far from holy, but the trip would set her on a path she could never have foreseen.

Upon reaching Jerusalem, Mary's curiosity led her to the Church of the Holy Sepulchre, where the relic of the True Cross was displayed. She followed the crowd, attempting to enter the sacred space, but found herself inexplicably repelled. An invisible force stopped her in her tracks, as though the very air around her had become an impenetrable wall. Time seemed to stand still as she realized the weight of her sins had barred her from entering this holy place. For the first time in her life, Mary was confronted with the reality of her soul's condition.

In the shadow of the church, she saw an icon of the Theotokos, the Mother of God. Falling to her knees, she wept bitterly, her tears washing away years of defiance and pride. In that moment of utter brokenness, she cried out to the Virgin Mary, pleading for forgiveness and guidance. She promised to leave behind her life of sin and follow wherever God would lead her. Suddenly, a sense of peace washed over her, and when she attempted to enter the church again, the unseen barrier was gone. She stepped inside, trembling with awe and gratitude, and venerated the relic of the Cross with a heart newly awakened to the grace of God.

As she left the church, Mary felt the stirrings of a divine call drawing her far from the temptations of the world. She crossed the Jordan River into the barren wilderness, armed only with three loaves of bread and an unshakable determination to begin a life of repentance. The desert, with its scorching heat by day and freezing cold by night, became her crucible, a place of both profound suffering and unimaginable transformation.

For the first seventeen years in the desert, Mary battled the demons of her past. The cravings for food, drink, and the carnal pleasures she had once delighted in clawed at her soul. She described the torment of her memories, the faces and voices of her former lovers haunting her mind like phantoms. Her body grew gaunt and weathered, her skin darkened by the relentless sun, and yet her spirit grew stronger with each passing trial. Her tears mingled with the dust, her prayers ascending to heaven like incense.

In time, the fiery temptations that had once plagued her began to fade. Mary entered into a profound communion with God, her soul blossoming in the isolation of the desert. She lived without worldly comforts, nourished only by the Eucharist, which she received once a year from a traveling priest. Her heart, once hardened by sin, became soft and radiant with divine love.

Decades passed in this hidden life of prayer and asceticism until, one day, a monk named Zosimas encountered her in the wilderness. Zosimas, a holy man in his own right, was awestruck by the sight of Mary, whose body was so transformed by her ascetic struggle that she seemed more like a creature of heaven than of earth. She shared her story with him, speaking of her conversion and her years in the desert, and begged him to bring her the Eucharist the following year.

When Zosimas returned as promised, he found Mary praying on the banks of the Jordan River. Miraculously, she walked across the water to receive the Body and Blood of Christ. It was the culmination of a life wholly surrendered to God. She asked Zosimas to return one year later, but when he did, he found her lifeless body, lying as though in peaceful repose. Written in the sand beside her was a note requesting burial and revealing that she had passed away immediately after receiving the Eucharist.

Zosimas buried her with great reverence, marveling at the miraculous transformation of a woman who had once been enslaved by sin but was now a shining example of God's boundless mercy and grace. Her story spread throughout the Church, becoming a timeless testament to the power of repentance and the possibility of redemption, no matter how far one has strayed.

Saint Mary of Egypt's life calls us to look beyond our past mistakes and embrace the mercy of a God who is always ready to welcome us home. Her journey from the depths of sin to the heights of holiness is not just a tale of personal redemption; it is an invitation to all who feel lost, weary, or unworthy. In her life, we see the truth that God's grace can reach even the darkest corners of the human soul, transforming them into vessels of His light. For those who struggle, Saint Mary stands as a witness to the hope and renewal found in surrendering to the love of Christ.

African Art, Byzantium, and the Shared Cultural Heritage

The connections between Africa and the Orthodox Christian tradition are not only spiritual but also artistic and cultural. Art history has long emphasized the glories of the Byzantine Empire (circa 330–1453), but less known are the profound artistic contributions of North Africa, Egypt, Nubia, Ethiopia, and other powerful African kingdoms whose pivotal interactions with Byzantium had a lasting impact on the Mediterranean world.

From the vibrant Coptic icons of Egypt to the intricate metalwork of Nubia and the illuminated manuscripts of Ethiopia, African artists made substantial contributions to the development of Christian art and culture. These artworks, rarely seen in public, tell the story of a rich and diverse heritage that shaped not only the Mediterranean world but also the broader Christian tradition.

The exhibition "Africa & Byzantium" was on display at the Metropolitan Museum of Art from November 2023 to March 2024 and at the Cleveland Museum of Art from April to July 2024. The exhibit showcased these masterworks, highlighting Africa's central role in international networks of trade and cultural exchange. From mosaic and sculpture to pottery and religious manuscripts, this exhibition sheds new light on the staggering artistic achievements of medieval Africa and offers a more complete history of the vibrant, multiethnic societies of north and east Africa that shaped the artistic, economic, and cultural life of Byzantium and beyond.

Reflections on a Shared Story of Faith

For African American Orthodox Christians, these stories and artistic legacies are more than just historical artifacts; they are a bridge connecting modern seekers to their ancient heritage. They remind us that Orthodoxy is not confined to any one race or culture but is a universal faith that embraces all who seek the truth. The icons of Saint Cyprian, Saint Moses, and Saint Mary of Egypt serve as windows into a spiritual world that transcends time and place, inviting us to join a communion of saints that stretches across continents and centuries.

Moving Forward: The Fellowship of St. Moses the Black and the Future of African American Orthodoxy

Today, the Fellowship of St. Moses the Black continues its work of reaching out to African Americans, offering Orthodoxy as a path to healing and transformation. Reflecting on my own journey, I see that the path to Orthodoxy is not always easy, but it is always worth it. It is a journey that leads to a deeper understanding of who we are, who God is, and the love that God has for each of us.

Through the stories shared on platforms like Ancient Faith Radio and YouTube, a growing chorus affirms that Orthodoxy is not confined by race or culture. These voices remind us that faith is a universal language, spoken in every human heart that seeks the Divine.

The Art and Architecture of Orthodox America

The Church as Icon

Orthodox churches in America, like their counterparts worldwide, are more than mere buildings; they are sacred spaces that embody and reflect the heavenly reality. From the soaring domes that mirror the firmament to the icons that serve as windows to eternity, these churches are designed to lift the hearts and minds of the faithful toward God. The art and architecture of Orthodox churches in America provide a profound expression of theology through visual beauty, connecting the earthly with the divine and offering an invitation to experience the sacred.

Orthodox Architecture: A Synthesis of Tradition and Modernity

The architecture of Orthodox churches in America is a blend of traditional Eastern Christian forms and modern innovations, with each structure embodying the theological truths of the

Orthodox faith. One of the most remarkable examples of this synthesis is Holy Trinity Russian Orthodox Cathedral in Chicago, designed by Louis Sullivan, a pioneering figure in American architecture. Built in the Ukrainian Village, this cathedral appears as though it has been transported from a small village in southern Russia. Its modest yet intricate design reflects the simplicity and intimacy of the rural churches that inspired it, while its ornate interior, filled with incense and icons, creates a space that invites contemplation and prayer.

Sullivan, who designed only two houses of worship in his career, captured the essence of Orthodox architecture in Holy Trinity Cathedral. He avoided the monumental styles typical of northern Russian churches and chose instead a provincial style, which resonated with the immigrant community that built it. The result is a church that feels both humble and sacred, a place where heaven and earth meet in a uniquely American context.

Another significant figure in the field of Orthodox architecture is Andrew Gould, whose work is dedicated to reviving and advancing traditional Orthodox architectural styles in North America. Gould, an architect, liturgical designer, and founder of New World Byzantine Studios, has been at the forefront of this movement, emphasizing the importance of creating spaces that serve as true icons of the heavenly reality. His designs incorporate elements of classical Byzantine architecture—such as domes, arches, and icon screens—while also responding to the local environment and cultural context.

Gould's approach is evident in his design for St. John the Baptist Orthodox Church in Charleston, South Carolina, where he transformed an ordinary commercial building into a sacred space by adding a beautifully crafted iconostasis, frescoes, and a bell tower that echoes the architectural language of Byzantine and Russian Orthodox churches. His work demonstrates that Orthodox architecture can thrive in contemporary America without losing its connection to its ancient roots.

Andrew Gould's contributions to Orthodox architecture in America are rooted in a profound understanding of the sacred and the beautiful. As an architect and designer, Gould believes that Orthodox churches should serve as icons themselves, drawing the faithful into a deeper experience of the divine. His work emphasizes the importance of creating spaces that are both beautiful and meaningful, spaces that reflect the glory of God and the mystery of the faith.

One of Gould's most significant projects is the Holy Ascension Orthodox Church in Charleston, South Carolina, where he used traditional Byzantine architectural elements, such as a large central dome and an iconostasis, to create a space that feels both ancient and timeless. His use of local materials and craftsmanship also reflects his commitment to creating churches that are not only beautiful but also sustainable and rooted in their local context.

Gould's work demonstrates a deep respect for tradition and a desire to create churches that are truly Orthodox in spirit and form. His designs are characterized by their attention to detail, their use of light and color, and their ability to create a sense of sacred space. By blending traditional Orthodox elements with modern architectural practices, Gould has helped to shape a new generation of Orthodox churches in America that are both beautiful and deeply meaningful.

The Role of Iconography: Theology in Color

Iconography is central to Orthodox worship, providing a visual theology that speaks directly to the soul. Icons are not mere decorations; they are sacred images that serve as windows to the divine, inviting the viewer into a deeper communion with God. In Orthodox churches across America, the work of skilled iconographers continues this tradition, ensuring that each church becomes a space where the faithful can encounter the divine.

A masterpiece of iconography has recently been completed at St. Seraphim of Sarov Orthodox Church in Santa Rosa, California. The dome, painted by Fr. Patrick Doolan, a renowned iconographer trained by Leonid Ouspensky, and his assistant, Fr. Moses, exemplifies the revival of traditional iconographic methods in America. Their work, done in true fresco, captures the spiritual essence of Orthodox theology in vibrant colors and profound symbolism. The dome, adorned with images of Christ Pantocrator, angels, and saints, draws the eyes upward, encouraging contemplation of the heavenly realm.

Similarly, Heather Mackean, a seventy-year-old iconographer who has painted various churches across the United States for over forty-five years, exemplifies the devotion and discipline required in this sacred art. Her work at the Annunciation Orthodox Church in Santa Maria, California, reflects her deep understanding of iconography as a visual language that proclaims the scripture and tradition of the Church. "In the Orthodox Church, the focus is not on the artist but on the work," Mackean explains, "because iconography is a visual language that proclaims the scripture and tradition of the Church without using words."

Orthodox Churches Through the Eyes of Western Artists

Orthodox churches have rarely been the subject of Western fine art, but the few paintings that exist offer a unique glimpse into the spiritual beauty of these sacred spaces. One of the most notable examples is the work of John Singer Sargent, an American painter known for his portraits and watercolors. Sargent's paintings of Byzantine churches reveal an extraordinary sensitivity to their unique beauty. His depictions of the interior of Hagia Sophia, for example, convey the subtle luster of worn marble, the fiery flash of a sunbeam on gold tesserae, and the ponderous quiet of an empty church in the early morning.

Sargent's work demonstrates the ability of naturalistic painting to capture the atmosphere and ethos of Orthodox churches in a way that photographs often cannot. These paintings offer a visual experience that feels almost prayerful, capturing the essence of these sacred spaces in a manner that resonates deeply with viewers. The subtle beauty of real materiality, as seen in Sargent's work, illustrates how Orthodox art can transform ordinary materials into something holy and transcendent.

The Symbolic World: The Work of Jonathan Pageau

Jonathan Pageau, an Orthodox icon carver and speaker, has brought a unique perspective to the world of Orthodox art through his exploration of symbolism and meaning. Pageau's work focuses on the deeper significance of icons and religious imagery, offering insights into how these symbols connect to the spiritual and material worlds.

Pageau's approach is rooted in the belief that icons and other sacred images are not just representations but participations in the divine reality. His carvings and writings explore how Orthodox art reflects the symbolic order of the universe, drawing connections between the material and spiritual worlds. For Pageau, the patterns and symbols found in Orthodox art are a way of seeing the world through a sacred lens, where every detail has meaning and purpose.

His work in the field of Orthodox iconography emphasizes the importance of understanding the deeper symbolism inherent in religious art. By exploring themes such as the cosmic order, the hierarchy of angels, and the sacred geometry of the universe, Pageau helps to illuminate the rich symbolic language of Orthodox art and its power to reveal the divine mysteries.

Conclusion: Art as Testament

The art and architecture of Orthodox America are a testament to the rich and diverse traditions that have shaped the Orthodox Church worldwide. From the humble beauty of Holy Trinity Russian Orthodox Cathedral in Chicago to the intricate iconography of St. Seraphim of Sarov in Santa Rosa, each church stands as an icon of the heavenly reality, inviting the faithful to enter into a deeper communion with God.

Through the work of architects like Andrew Gould and iconographers like Heather MacKean and Jonathan Pageau, the American Orthodox Church continues to create spaces that are both beautiful and meaningful, spaces that reflect the glory of God and the mystery of the faith. Whether through the revival of traditional Byzantine styles, the adaptation of local architectural forms, or the exploration of new symbolic languages, these artists and architects are helping to shape a new chapter in the history of Orthodox art and architecture, one that honors the past while looking boldly toward the future.

Holy Assumption Monastery in Calistoga, California

Holy Places and Pilgrimage in America

It was a crisp, clear morning in early 2022 when my wife, Lesa, and I attended a Divine Liturgy at St. John the Theologian Orthodox Church in Tempe, Arizona. We had come to celebrate our anniversary by immersing ourselves in the spiritual richness of the Orthodox faith. The church was filled with the scent of incense and the gentle glow of candlelight, a reminder of the Light of Christ.

After the liturgy, we felt a quiet joy as we set out on our journey to St. Anthony's Monastery in Florence, Arizona, a spiritual oasis founded by Blessed Elder Ephraim. The drive took us deeper into the heart of the Sonoran Desert, where the landscape shifted from bustling city streets to the serene expanse of the desert, framed by the distant silhouette of mountains.

Arriving at the monastery in the early afternoon, we were greeted by the whitewashed walls and terracotta domes that stood out against the backdrop of the arid wilderness. As we stepped onto the grounds, we felt an immediate sense of peace, a stillness that seemed to echo the deep quiet within our hearts. The gardens, filled with olive trees and fragrant blooms, enveloped us in their beauty, and the sound of the church bell called us to explore the sacred space further.

Our visit began with a walk through the various chapels, each with its unique character and sanctity. We spent time in the chapel where the relics of Blessed Elder Ephraim were kept, feeling the powerful presence of his holy life and the countless prayers offered there. The chapels were simple yet profoundly adorned, each icon a window into the divine. The atmosphere was thick with prayer, and we moved quietly, mindful of the sanctity of the place.

A Day of Pilgrimage and Reflection

That evening, as we left the monastery grounds, we felt a deep sense of connection to the holy men and women who have devoted their lives to God in this remote desert sanctuary. The following day, our journey continued north to Sedona, a place known for its stunning red rock formations and spiritual energy. The natural beauty of the rocks, carved by wind and water over millennia, seemed to speak of the divine artistry of creation.

We marveled at the power of the energy vortexes, which many believe hold spiritual significance. The landscape around us felt alive, imbued with a sacred presence that resonated deeply within our souls. We spent hours exploring the trails, feeling the grounding energy of the earth beneath our feet and the vast sky above.

From Sedona, we continued to the Grand Canyon, a marvel of natural wonder that left us speechless. Standing on the edge of the canyon, we gazed out over the vast expanse, its layers of rock telling the story of millions of years. The sheer magnitude and beauty of the canyon took our breath away, a reminder of the infinite creativity of God's handiwork. It was a moment of awe and reverence, a true encounter with the grandeur of creation.

Monasteries, Cathedrals, and Churches as Centers of Spiritual Renewal

Orthodox monasteries, cathedrals, and churches across America serve as vital centers of spiritual renewal, places where the faithful come to encounter the divine in a tangible way. These holy places, scattered throughout the country, offer sanctuaries of peace, prayer, and reflection. Each one is a unique expression of the ancient Christian tradition, made manifest in the New World.

Life-Giving Spring Monastery: A Hidden Gem in the Sierra Nevadas

In August 2018, while on a work assignment in Fresno, California, I had an unexpected opportunity to visit Life-Giving Spring Monastery in Dunlap. With an extra day off, I decided to take a detour to this small Greek Orthodox monastery nestled in the Sierra Nevada foothills. As I drove up the winding road, the air grew cooler, and the scent of pine trees filled my senses. The monastery appeared like a hidden gem amid the towering sequoias, a place of profound beauty and tranquility.

Upon arrival, I was warmly welcomed by Mother Markella and the other nuns, whose kindness made me feel at home. The monastery's white stone buildings with red-tiled roofs stood out against the dense forest, creating a sense of timelessness. The chapel, filled with the flickering light of oil lamps and richly adorned with icons, served as the heart of the monastery, a place where heaven seemed to touch earth.

I joined the sisters for the Divine Liturgy and experienced the power of their prayerful chanting. The atmosphere was filled with an almost tangible sense of peace, the air thick with the prayers of those who had lived, prayed, and worshiped in this sacred place for years. Walking through the monastery gardens afterward, I felt a deep sense of renewal, as if the very earth was blessed by the presence of these devoted women.

Holy Assumption Monastery: A Vineyard of Faith in Napa Valley

Another memorable pilgrimage was to Holy Assumption Monastery in Calistoga, California, nestled amidst the vineyards of Napa Valley. On the Feast of the Dormition of the Theotokos, I joined a group of pilgrims in celebrating this important feast day at the monastery. The beauty of the setting, with its chapels adorned with icons and filled with the fragrance of incense, added to the sacredness of the occasion.

We were welcomed by the nuns, who guided us through the day's services, which included Matins, Divine Liturgy, and a procession around the grounds. The small chapel, with its wooden chairs and simple iconography, radiated a quiet beauty that seemed to draw everyone into a state of deep prayer. The hymns sung by the sisters resonated through the chapel, their voices blending in perfect harmony, creating a sense of unity and peace.

After the services, we gathered in the monastery's gardens for a meal prepared by the sisters. The hospitality and warmth of the monastic community were palpable, a reflection of their commitment to living the Gospel through love and service. The day was filled with prayers, hymns, and fellowship—a time of deep spiritual reflection and joy.

Holy Assumption Monastery is home to the St. Peter the Aleut Icon that miraculously washed ashore at Fort Ross as described in the *American Orthodox* book. Abbess Melania, Mother Macrina, and Mother Tabitha were featured in the film.

The Pilgrimage of 2024: A Journey through Orthodox Los Angeles

In 2024, my journey continued with a pilgrimage tour of Orthodox churches, cathedrals, and shrines in the Los Angeles area. This journey was filled with encounters that deepened my faith and brought me closer to the heart of Orthodoxy in America.

St. Andrew Orthodox Church: Meeting Father Josiah Trenham

One of the notable stops on this tour was St. Andrew Orthodox Church in Riverside, where I had the opportunity to meet Father Josiah Trenham, the well-known priest, author, and the founder of Patristic Nectar Publications. The church, modeled after the thirteenth-century World Heritage Site of St.

Catherine's Monastery in Thessaloniki, Greece, was completed in 2011 as the first Byzantine-style Orthodox Christian church in Riverside.

Inside, the iconography is a testament to the rich tradition of Orthodox Christian art. The walls are adorned with hand-painted icons created by Orthodox iconographer monks from Buena Vista, Colorado. These icons, depicting scenes from the life of Christ, His miracles, parables, and hundreds of saints, cover every available surface. When completed, this iconographic scheme will be one of the most elaborate in the United States, leaving no wall space unadorned. The images are vibrant, alive with color and detail, and draw the faithful into a deeper contemplation of the mysteries of the faith.

Father Josiah's ministry through Patristic Nectar Publications has made a significant impact on Orthodox Christians worldwide, providing access to theological lectures, homilies, and books that deepen understanding of the faith. His passion for Orthodoxy and commitment to teaching the Church Fathers' wisdom was evident in our conversations. As I listened to him speak about Christ, I felt inspired by his dedication to spreading the gospel in a way that resonates with both traditional and contemporary audiences.

Holy Transfiguration Cathedral and Holy Virgin Mary Cathedral: Sacred Spaces in Los Angeles

My pilgrimage also took me to Holy Transfiguration Cathedral in Los Angeles, a church that has long served as a beacon of Orthodoxy in the city. The cathedral's striking interior, filled with icons and mosaics, created an atmosphere of prayer and contemplation. I spent time here in quiet reflection, soaking in the beauty of the sacred art that adorned every corner of the space.

From there, I visited Holy Virgin Mary Cathedral, a place with a unique historical significance. It was here that the famous Russian-born actress Natalie Wood was married, and where the faithful still come to pray and seek the intercession of the Mother of God. I obtained blessed holy oil from the miraculous icon of the Theotokos, Rescuer of the Perishing. As I stood before this icon, I felt a profound connection to the countless others who had come to this place in search of comfort, healing, and hope.

Saint Sophia Greek Orthodox Cathedral: A Jewel in Los Angeles

Saint Sophia Greek Orthodox Cathedral, another stop on my pilgrimage, is one of the most unusual churches in Los Angeles. The cathedral's stunning architecture, with its massive domes and intricate frescoes, reflects the grandeur of Byzantine tradition. The interior is filled with light, streaming through stained glass windows, casting colorful patterns on the marble floors. The icons and mosaics that adorn the walls tell the story of Christ and His saints, drawing the faithful into the mystery of the divine.

Here I spent time praying and reflecting, feeling the weight of history and the presence of the holy in every detail of the church's design.

St. Nectarios Shrine: A Place of Miracles

The final stop on my pilgrimage was the St. Nectarios Shrine in Covina. Upon arriving, we visited the relics of St. Nectarios before the films *Sacred Alaska* and *Amphilochios* were screened. The atmosphere was filled with reverence and anticipation as we gathered to witness these inspiring stories of faith and devotion.

I was able to visit St. Nectarios Shrine again the following Sunday afternoon, when they provided a vespers service and anointing with blessed oil from the lamp above the relics of St. Nectarios. The experience was deeply moving, and I felt a profound sense of peace and healing. St. Nectarios, featured in the award-winning film *Man of God*, continues to inspire countless people with his life and miracles, and I was grateful for the opportunity to draw closer to his holy presence.

Flames of Uncertainty: The Los Angeles Fires of January 2025

The road to Los Angeles, a city forever entwined with ambition and despair, now cuts through a fiery wasteland. Smoke claws at the horizon, painting the skies in apocalyptic hues as the once-vibrant hills of Malibu and Eaton Canyon smolder. The fires began innocuously enough, a flicker here, a spark there, but by January 7, the Feast of the Nativity of Christ (Julian Calendar), they had erupted into an uncontrollable inferno. This dual catastrophe—the Pacific Palisades/Malibu fire and the Eaton Canyon blaze—has, at this writing, ravaged over 38,000 acres, devoured 19,000 structures and vehicles, and claimed 24 lives.

It is, by every measure, the most devastating fire in Los Angeles history.

As I write this in January 2025, the fires continue their relentless march, only 14 percent and 33 percent contained, respectively. The winds, those unpredictable accomplices of destruction, have returned today, fueling the flames and dashing the hopes of exhausted firefighters. Entire neighborhoods lie in ruins, reduced to skeletal frames and ash-strewn streets. More than 150,000 residents have fled, their lives upended, and thousands more stand ready to evacuate at a moment's notice. The usual winter rains, those merciful torrents that bring life to parched California soil, have failed to arrive, leaving the region dry and treacherously vulnerable.

Despite this chaos, a peculiar paradox unfolds in the city. Central Los Angeles and the San Fernando Valley remain untouched by the inferno. Their skies remain an unbroken blue, as if mocking the tragedy playing out on their fringes. Life here continues with only minor disruptions—short power outages and gusty winds. The ash, carried by southerly breezes, dissipates over the Pacific, sparing the metropolis the choking haze that so often accompanies such disasters.

The Resilience of Faith

Amid this unfolding tragedy, the Orthodox Christian community of Los Angeles stands as a testament to the enduring power of faith. Remarkably, not a single Orthodox church has suffered structural damage, though the Pokrov Church (ROCOR) in Hollywood came dangerously close to evacuation when flames from the Sunset Fire crept toward its doors on January 9. The miraculous preservation of these sacred spaces offers a glimmer of hope in a landscape marked by despair.

Prayers for deliverance echoed through the city's Orthodox parishes on Sunday, January 12. Litanies rose like incense, mingling with the smoke-filled air as the faithful implored divine intervention. At the Transfiguration Cathedral, a moleben was served before a copy of the Los Angeles icon of the Mother of God, a symbol of the city's spiritual heartbeat. Across town at St. Innocent Church, a prayer for rain was offered before the Vladimir icon, a relic that had survived a previous fire—a silent witness to resilience and renewal.

Acts of mercy sprang from this community like water from a hidden spring. At Holy Virgin Mary Cathedral, parishioners, led by chef Markell Titov, prepared and delivered hot meals to firefighters and displaced residents. These simple yet profound acts of kindness illuminated the darkness, a reminder that even amidst destruction, the light of compassion endures.

A Personal Toll

The fires spared few from their reach, and the Orthodox community was no exception. On January 8, Archpriest Janis Terauds, assistant rector of Holy Transfiguration Cathedral, was involved in a serious car accident while en route to serve the Divine Liturgy. Disabled traffic lights, casualties of power outages, turned intersections into battlegrounds. A speeding truck collided with Father Janis's vehicle, leaving him hospitalized. Though he recovered and was released, his trials were far from over; he and his family were forced to evacuate their home shortly thereafter.

Father Janis's story is emblematic of the challenges faced by countless Angelenos during this crisis. It is a story of disruption and perseverance, of faith tested and renewed. His resilience mirrors that of the city itself—a place that, despite its scars, refuses to yield to despair.

An Echo of the Past

As I reflect on this ongoing disaster, I am reminded of another calamity etched into memory: September 11, 2001. On that fateful day, some Orthodox Christians employed at the World Trade Center were spared by what could only be described as divine providence. By God's grace, they did not show up for work that morning, escaping the tragedy that unfolded. Similarly, in this firestorm, a sense of divine mercy permeates the narrative. The preservation of churches, the miraculous survival of icons, and the relative safety of parishioners—all point to a higher hand at work.

Yet the fires also serve as a sobering reminder of humanity's vulnerability. The vast destruction, the lives lost, and the sheer unpredictability of nature underscore our fragile existence. They compel us to turn inward, to seek meaning amidst chaos, and to find solace in the eternal.

A City's Cross to Bear

Los Angeles has always been a city of contrasts—a glittering facade masking an undercurrent of struggle. The fires have stripped away that veneer, revealing a raw, unfiltered reality. Yet, in this crucible of fire and ash, a deeper truth emerges: the indomitable spirit of a community bound by faith, compassion, and resilience.

As the flames continue their relentless advance, we pray not only for rain but for renewal—for a city that will rise from the ashes, stronger and more united. We pray for those who have lost homes and loved ones, for the firefighters who risk their lives, and for a world that seems increasingly fragile.

This chapter of Los Angeles's history is still being written. As we navigate its unfolding, may we find strength in the stories of those who persevere, and may we carry their lessons into our own lives. For in the face of destruction, it is our shared humanity, our faith, and our hope that will see us through.

The Future of Orthodoxy in America

A New Dawn in the Church

The first light of dawn is breaking over the city as I stand outside Elevation of the Holy Cross Orthodox Church in Sacramento, watching as parishioners arrive for the early morning Divine Liturgy. The air is crisp, and there is a sense of anticipation in the air. As I step inside, I am struck by the diversity of the congregation—people of all ages, ethnicities, and backgrounds gathered in prayer. I find myself filled with hope for the future of Orthodoxy in America, even as I recognize the challenges that lie ahead.

Reflections on Growth, Challenges, and Opportunities

Orthodoxy in America stands at a crossroads, facing both opportunities and obstacles as it looks to the future. In recent years, the Church has seen a resurgence of interest, particularly among younger generations seeking a spiritual path that offers depth, mystery, and a sense of connection to something greater than themselves. This growth has been driven by a variety of factors: the beauty and mystery of the Orthodox liturgy, the timeless teachings of the Church Fathers, and the sense of belonging that comes from being part of a close-knit community.

However, this growth is not without its challenges. The Orthodox Church in America is diverse, comprising multiple jurisdictions—Greek, Russian, Serbian, Antiochian, and others—each with its own traditions, languages, and customs. This diversity is both a strength and a potential source of division. As Orthodoxy grows in America, it must navigate the delicate balance of honoring its rich cultural heritage while also creating a unified witness to the gospel.

There are also external challenges. The Church must contend with an increasingly secular culture that often views religion with skepticism or hostility. As society becomes more polarized, the Church is called to be a beacon of peace and reconciliation, offering a different path—one rooted in love, humility, and forgiveness.

The Role of Saints, Miracles, and the Faithful

The future of Orthodoxy in America will be shaped by its saints, its miracles, and its faithful. The stories of modern saints like St. John Maximovitch, St. Herman of Alaska, and St. Sebastian of Jackson inspire the faithful and serve as a reminder that God is active and present in our world. Miraculous events, such as the myrrh-streaming icons of North America, continue to draw people to the faith, offering tangible signs of God's love and grace.

But perhaps most importantly, the future of Orthodoxy in America will be shaped by the everyday saints—the ordinary men and women who live their faith with sincerity, devotion, and love. It is through their prayers, their actions, and their witness that the Church will grow and thrive. The faithful are the backbone of the Church, the ones who build it up through their daily acts of kindness, their dedication to prayer, and their willingness to serve.

Looking Ahead: Hope and Challenge

Looking to the future, I am filled with hope. I have seen firsthand the power of faith in the lives of countless people, from the recent converts in small mission parishes to the cradle Orthodox who have lived their faith for generations. I have witnessed the growth of vibrant communities, the establishment of new monasteries, and the renewal of old parishes. I have met people whose lives have been transformed by the encounter with Christ in His Church.

Yet I am also aware of the challenges that lie ahead. The Church must continue to find ways to reach out to those who are searching for God in a culture that often seems to have forgotten Him. It must find ways to bridge the gaps between different jurisdictions and build a unified Orthodox presence in America. It must remain true to its ancient teachings while finding new ways to engage with a modern world.

As we look to the future, we must remember that the Church is not a static institution but a living, breathing body—a family united by faith. It is our responsibility to continue the work of the apostles, to share the gospel with those who have not yet heard it, and to be living witnesses of Christ in all that we do.

Epilogue

CONTINUING THE PILGRIMAGE

Discovering the Ancient Faith in a Modern World

The Pacific wind whipped through the tall redwoods, carrying the scent of salt from the nearby ocean. At Fort Ross, the fog rolled in like a soft blanket, draping itself over the ancient wooden structures that once stood as a gateway to a new world for Russian explorers and Orthodox missionaries. I stood among friends, parishioners, Orthodox clergy, and a film crew, surrounded by prayers, the quiet click of cameras, and the hum of anticipation. We were there to honor St. Peter the Aleut, the young martyr who gave his life for Christ in this place, and to celebrate the many saints whose presence has transformed America.

The chanting of hymns in multiple languages filled the air, a tapestry of faith stretching across continents and centuries. Here, in this remote outpost on the California coast, the ancient faith of Orthodoxy felt as vibrant and alive as ever, continuing its timeless journey across the American landscape.

As I watched, I felt a deep connection to those who had walked this path before us—St. Peter the Aleut, St. Innocent, St. John the Wonderworker, and others who brought the light of Orthodoxy to these shores. Their stories were not distant history but an ongoing narrative, a living faith that still inspires, challenges, and transforms us today.

The Living Faith: Saints, Miracles, and the Ongoing Story of Orthodoxy in America

Throughout this book, we have traveled together across the vast landscape of America, tracing the footsteps of saints, witnessing miracles, and discovering the profound beauty of Orthodox Christianity as it takes root in this land. We have explored lives touched by the divine—the saints whose stories of sacrifice and holiness inspire us to live with greater purpose and conviction. We have encountered miracles that defy explanation, reminding us of God's constant presence, intervening in our lives in profound ways. And we have witnessed the living faith of countless Orthodox Christians who, in their daily struggles and triumphs, bear witness to the truth of the gospel.

This journey has revealed a Church that is both ancient and ever new, a faith that embraces the fullness of life and calls us to holiness amid our everyday challenges, offering hope and healing in a world that desperately needs both.

A Call to Holiness

The saints, miracles, and holy places we have explored are not just historical landmarks; they are signposts pointing us toward our spiritual destiny. They remind us that we are all called to be

Epilogue

saints, to live lives of holiness, courage, and love, to bear witness to the light of Christ in our own time and place. Their stories are an invitation to continue this journey, to seek out the sacred in our lives, and to become part of this ongoing story of faith.

As we stand at Fort Ross, celebrating the Divine Liturgy under the wide California sky, there is a deep sense of hope for the future of Orthodoxy in America. The faces around me—young and old, from every race and background—reflect the diversity and vitality of a Church that continues to grow, adapt, and flourish in this land. The story of Orthodoxy in America is still being written, and each of us has a part to play.

An Invitation

The road ahead is a pilgrimage, not a destination. Each step offers new challenges, new questions, and new opportunities to discover the depth and beauty of Orthodoxy. This journey, which began for me many years ago, has led to unexpected places, encounters with saints, and connections with holy people and communities that have transformed my life.

I offer you an invitation: Come and see. Step onto this path of discovery. The ancient faith is alive in the most unexpected corners of the modern world—in small mission parishes tucked away in suburban neighborhoods, in majestic cathedrals that echo with the prayers of generations, and in the quiet stillness of monasteries where the heart finds rest.

The call to holiness is not about perfection but about a life of repentance, humility, and love. It is a call to face the light of Christ, to allow His love to transform us from within, and to be saints in our time, carrying the torch of faith to new generations.

May the grace of our Lord Jesus Christ, the love of God the Father, and the communion of the Holy Spirit be with you as you take up this call. The story of this journey is just beginning, and it belongs to all of us.

Appendix

A GUIDE TO PILGRIMAGE SITES AND HOLY PLACES IN AMERICA

Recommended Monasteries, Churches, and Sacred Sites to Visit

Orthodoxy in America offers a wealth of sacred places that invite pilgrims to encounter the divine. Here is a guide to a few of the most significant monasteries, churches, and pilgrimage sites across the country, each with its unique history, beauty, and spiritual significance. You may find many more in your own region.

Monasteries

St. Anthony's Monastery (Florence, Arizona). Founded by Elder Ephraim, this men's monastery is a spiritual oasis in the Sonoran Desert. Visitors can participate in the daily cycle of services, walk the beautifully landscaped gardens, and receive spiritual counsel from the monastic community.

St. Herman of Alaska Monastery (Platina, California). Nestled in the mountains of Northern California, this men's monastery offers a peaceful retreat for those seeking quiet and prayer. The monastery is known for its connection to Father Seraphim Rose, whose grave is a site of pilgrimage.

Holy Assumption Monastery (Calistoga, California). This beautiful and unique women's monastery in the Napa Valley is located just a few blocks off the main street through Calistoga, California. The nuns make the most of their limited land through terraced and raised gardens and have created an absolutely beautiful haven for pilgrims and visitors. A large koi pond is a favorite with the town's schoolchildren (and with guests), but it's when one enters the chapel that one encounters the divine heart of the monastery, which includes a miraculous, self-renewing icon of St. Nicholas, and a wood-carved icon of St. Peter the Aleut which was revealed to a friend of the monastery as she walked along the Pacific coast, and saw it floating to the shore bathed in light.

Monastery of the Theotokos, the Life-Giving Spring (Dunlap, California). A women's monastery located in the Sierra Nevada foothills, known for its vibrant community and serene environment. Pilgrims can attend services, meet with the sisters, and find spiritual renewal in this sacred place.

Churches and Cathedrals
Holy Virgin Cathedral (San Francisco, California). This Russian Orthodox cathedral, dedicated to the icon of the Mother of

Appendix

God Joy of All Who Sorrow, is known for its stunning mosaics and as the resting place of the relics of St. John Maximovitch. A center of spiritual life in the Bay Area, it offers daily services and opportunities for confession and spiritual guidance.

St. Sava Serbian Orthodox Church (Jackson, California). The first Serbian Orthodox church in the Western Hemisphere, this historic site is a place of pilgrimage for those seeking to connect with the roots of Orthodoxy in America. The church houses the relics of St. Sebastian of Jackson and offers a glimpse into the rich history of Serbian Orthodox Christians in America.

Elevation of the Holy Cross Orthodox Church (Sacramento, California). A vibrant community with services in English, welcoming converts from various backgrounds. Known for its beautiful liturgical life and strong emphasis on outreach and education.

St. Nicholas Russian Orthodox Cathedral (New York, New York). Located in the heart of Manhattan, this cathedral is a spiritual refuge in the bustling city. Known for its rich liturgical tradition and stunning architecture, it offers a glimpse of the beauty of Russian Orthodoxy.

Sacred Sites

St. Tikhon's Monastery (Waymart, Pennsylvania). The oldest Orthodox monastery in America, founded in 1905, and a center of pilgrimage and spiritual life. The monastery grounds include a seminary, a museum, and beautiful chapels, attracting visitors from all over the world.

Fort Ross (Sonoma County, California). The site of the first Orthodox church in California, established by Russian settlers in the nineteenth century. Pilgrims can explore the historic fort and visit the reconstructed chapel, which continues to be a place of prayer and commemoration.

Holy Trinity Monastery (Jordanville, New York). A spiritual and cultural center for Russian Orthodoxy in America, known for its seminary, publishing house, and beautiful grounds. Pilgrims can attend services, meet with the monks, and participate in retreats and educational programs.

Practical Information for Spiritual Seekers

» **Plan ahead:** Contact the monastery or church in advance to inquire about visiting hours, accommodations, and any specific guidelines for pilgrims.
» **Dress appropriately:** Modest attire is generally required when visiting monasteries and churches. Women may be asked to wear skirts and cover their heads; men should wear long pants and avoid sleeveless shirts.
» **Participate in services:** Attending services is an integral part of the pilgrimage experience. Be prepared for long services, especially at monasteries, and participate as much as you feel comfortable.
» **Respect the sacred space:** Remember that you are entering a holy place. Maintain a respectful demeanor, keep

Appendix

conversations quiet, and follow any instructions given by the clergy or monastic community.

Embark on your own journey, explore these sacred spaces, and open yourself to the spiritual riches that await. Each of these places offers a unique opportunity to draw closer to God, to experience His grace, and to deepen your faith in the ancient tradition of Orthodoxy.

About the Author

Robert John Hammond is a bestselling author, award-winning screenwriter, and visionary filmmaker whose work bridges the realms of history, faith, and storytelling. The creator of *American Orthodox: Finding the Ancient Faith in the Modern World* and producer of the upcoming *American Orthodox* documentary, he also edited and contributed to *Roads Less Traveled: Journeys to Orthodoxy*. His acclaimed books include *Life After Debt, Identity Theft, Transformed by Writing*, and the autobiographical novel *The Light*. Holding a Master of Fine Arts in Creative Writing, he has taught graduate-level screenwriting and penned the award-winning screenplay *DeMille*, based on his book *CB DeMille: The Man Who Invented Hollywood*. As a producer of numerous films, including the investigative documentary *Bohemian Grove*, Hammond crafts narratives that pulse with cinematic intensity, drawing readers and viewers into profound and transformative journeys.

www.ingramcontent.com/pod-product-compliance
Lightning Source LLC
Chambersburg PA
CBHW051837090426
42736CB00011B/1852